On-line Text Management

HyperText and Other Techniques

On-line text management

On-line Text Management

HyperText and Other Techniques

P. C. McGrew
W. D. McDaniel

Intertext Publications
McGraw-Hill Book Company

New York St. Louis San Francisco Auckland Bogotá
Hamburg London Madrid Mexico Milan Montreal
New Delhi Panama Paris São Paulo
Singapore Sidney Tokyo Toronto

Library of Congress Catalog Card Number 88-83707

Copyright © 1989 by P.C. McGrew and W.D. McDaniel. All rights reserved. Printed in the United States of America. Except as permitted under the United States Copyright Act of 1976, no part of this book may be reproduced or distributed in any form or by any means, or stored in a database or retrieval system without the prior written permission of the publisher.

10 9 8 7 6 5 4 3 2 1

ISBN 0-07-046263-1

Intertext Publications/Multiscience Press, Inc.
One Lincoln Plaza
New York, NY 10023

McGraw-Hill Book Company
1221 Avenue of the Americas
New York, NY 10020

*This one,
with love,
is dedicated to our families*

CONTENTS

PART 1: Introduction

Chapter 1:
    What Is an On-line Text Access System? ... 3

    Types of Text Access 4
        On-line Help 4
        Free-standing Text Environments 6
        Context-sensitive Text Environments 6
        Summary 7

    Why Implement an On-line System? 8

    When Do You Need an On-line Application? 9

Chapter 2:
    What Are the Benefits of an On-line System? 11

    Evaluating On-line Text 12

    Selling the Idea to Users 17

    Additional Considerations 20

    Caveats 20

Chapter 3:
    Establishing a Baseline: Terms and Concepts 23

    Storage Devices 24
        Virtual Storage 24
        On-line Storage 25
        Off-line Storage 27

    Other Hardware 28

	Terminals	29
	Displays	29
	Workstations	30
	Networks	30
	Scanners	31
	Software	32
	Interactive Computing Environments	33
	Access Methods	34
	Composition and Printing	35
	Compilers and Subprograms	37
	Organization of Information	39
	Document Organization	40
	Data Organization	41
	For MVS and VSE	41
	Database Organization	43
	System Organization	45
Chapter 4:	Minimum Mainframe Requirements	49
	CPU Power	51
	Storage Requirements	54
	Virtual Storage	54
	On-line Storage	55
	Near-line Storage	57
	Off-line Storage	58
	Terminals	60
	Text-only Terminals	60
	Color	61
	Graphics and WYSIWYG	61
	System Requirements Review	66

PART 2: Directions in Text Access

Chapter 5:
    Text Access Methods Yesterday and Today   71

    Error Messages 72

    Specific Text Mapping 74

    Context-sensitive Text Access 77
        On-line Tutorials 77
        Computer-based Instruction 79

    The Next Step 79

Chapter 6:
    New Approaches to Accessing Text 81

    New Presentation Methods 82

    Associative Navigation 84

    HyperText Systems 87

    HyperMedia 91

    Selecting the Access Method 94

Chapter 7:
    What Do You Want from Your Text Access System? 95

    Making More Information More Available . 96

    Reducing Information Dissemination Costs 98

    Evaluation Checklist 99

PART 3: Display Design

Chapter 8:
- Designing Screen Text Appearance 107
- Screen Environment Restrictions 108
  - Color 110
  - Mixed Case 110
  - Fonts and Highlighting 110
  - Screen Depth 111
- Other Hardware Restrictions 112

Chapter 9:
- Formatting the Presentation 115
- Capturing Text 116
  - Keying 116
  - Copying 117
  - Scanning 118
- Formatting the Text 119
  - Manual Formatting 122
  - Composing Text 123
  - Viewing Graphically Composed Text ... 124
  - Formatting for Windows 125
  - Who Is in Control? 127
  - Consistency 129

Chapter 10:
- Presentation Control 131
- What Are Windows? 132
- What Are Panels? 133
- Windows versus Panels 134

Selecting the Appropriate Presentation
Method 137

Windows: Tiling or Overlapping? 138
   Tiling Windows 138
   Overlapping Windows 139

Displaying Text on the Screen 140

Reading Screen Text 142

Interactive Text Perusal 143

Interactions with Others 143

Interacting with the Text 144

Ultimate Interactivity 146

PART 4: Text Member Source Design

Chapter 11:
   Evaluating Your Text Library 151

   Existing Libraries 152
      From Typewritten Masters 153
      From Floppy Disk 153
      On Your Host 154

   New Text Members 155
      Keying 156
      Scanning 156

   Just a Few More Questions 159

Chapter 12:
   Configuring Your Text Source 161

   Formatting Control—Where Should It Be? 162
   Profiles and Style Files 162

Formatting Differences: On-line vs.
Printed 164

How Big Should a Text Member Be? 164
Managing Multi-use Files 165
Configuring Main Document Files 167

Document Management 167
Naming Conventions 168
Automated Version Control 169

Creating Text Members 170

General Text 170

Heavily Formatted Text 172

Graphics 173

PART 5: Technical Considerations

Chapter 13:
Access to Text in Electronic Libraries ... 177

Physical Organization of Text as Data ... 178
Text Access Methods 178
Data Structures 179

Search and Retrieval Methods 184

Chapter 14:
Connecting and Relating Library Members 187

HyperText Interrelating Techniques 188
Link Management 190
Other HyperText Facilities 191

Traditional Interrelating Techniques 192
Bookmarking 193

Chapter 15:
Document Structures Within Electronic Libraries 195

Tree-structure Documents 196

Network Document Structures 198

Relationally Structured Documents 198

Linear Documents 198

HyperDocument Organization 200

Document Access Functions 201

Chapter 16:
Processor Considerations 203

Page Transition Time 204

Search Algorithms 205

Multi-tasking Processes 207

Graphics 207

WYSIWYG 208

APPENDICES

Appendix A:
Evaluation Checklist Review 213

Our On-line Environment 221

Appendix B:
Creating This Book 221

Appendix C:
Creating a Prototype On-line Text Environment 225

Appendix D:
　　　　Trademarks 229

　　　　Index 233

Preface

We created this book as an answer to all of those people who claim that the world of text access, retrieval, and manipulation for the mainframe computer user can never be as good or as user-friendly as the world of the personal computer or workstation user. With some thought to design and some thought to implementation, most of the intelligent user interfaces found in the smaller environments can be migrated to the mainframe, or can coexist across the mainframe and PC/workstation environments. This includes applications from on-line help facilities to simple access to reference text, from simple access to a text database to context-sensitive entry into a text database. You can have it all.

The Audience

We think this book is important for *anyone* involved in creating, managing, or using mainframe application environments. In some way, shape, or form all mainframe applications have text associated with them. They may manipulate text, produce text, or passively require that the user have access to off-line documents, such as user manuals, reference manuals, or implementation guides.

To make this book most helpful to the broadest number of people, we have tried to provide a fair amount of detail about the IBM/370 mainframe environment, especially in *Caveats*. This detail will be superfluous to very technical mainframe users, but should help non-technical managers and users to understand the complexities involved in developing and implementing an on-line text application.

Our Idea

Our idea is that mainframe users *can* have the speed and storage range of the large systems and yet work through a friendly and appealing user interface. We believe that this is a pioneering concept. Many computer users who begin to investigate ways to improve their environment are told that the applications and interfaces they would like cannot be handled effectively or efficiently in an IBM/370 mainframe architecture environment. By picking up this book you have begun the process of breaking through these myths. In this book we guide you through the step-by-step development of an on-line text display and management system.

We begin by defining the minimum environments and the basic jargon associated with text access, and then move into the nuts and bolts of building the best system for your environment. We provide guidelines for evaluating your environment to help you determine what type of on-line text retrieval and management environment you would like to create. And then we tell you how to do it.

We cover all of the facets, including the design of the system, creation and management of text files, and the type of programming required to make it all come together into a package. As you find out what is possible, you can make decisions about how basic or how sophisticated the system for your environment can and should be.

Out here, on the leading edge of mainframe computer applications, very little is impossible. We demonstrate how to build several different kinds of on-line text systems, ranging from the simple display of composed text, to more PC-like applications using windows and menus that incorporate associative navigation and hypertext information retrieval techniques.

Using This Book

Your path through the remainder of the book may take any of several directions. If you are primarily interested in the creation of the text to be used in an on-line system, you can concentrate your attention on Parts 3 and 4. If you are primarily interested in the programming requirements, concentrate your attention on Parts 3 and 5. If you require an overall understanding, read the entire book in the sequence presented.

Product Information

It would be impossible to create a book like this and not name quite a few products whose names are trademarked by their owners. To avoid the clutter than can occur on a page when one entry after another has a footnote associated with it, we have gathered all of the trademarked entities into an appendix, *Our On-line Environment*, and identified their owners. For more information on any of the products named, contact the vendors directly. If you have difficulty locating information, please contact the authors.

Acknowledgments

We must first thank our friends and colleagues who helped us define our ideas and provided feedback. We want to especially thank the following people for reading and critiquing drafts of the manuscript:

- **Carolyn Rosenberg, Manager of Documentation Systems, Candle Corporation, Los Angeles, CA**

    Carolyn has been our most enthusiastic supporter. She read drafts that were sometimes no more than a shell of an idea and shared her ideas with us. Her questions to us about what was and was not possible often helped us to break more ground toward our goal of creating a usable on-line text system using existing source files.

- **Frank Zdanowski, Senior Development Center Analyst, Kemper Group, Long Grove, IL**

    Frank is an old friend. From his vantage point in the development center of a large insurance provider, he provides a critical eye and an understanding of the requirements of end-users.

- **Annette Norris Bradford, Staff Information Planner, IBM, Kingston, NY**

    Annette is a new friend who has a common interest in technical communication in general and on-line text specifically. We met when she became the IBM representative to the Professional Development project at SHARE; from that moment on she became a valuable source of material drawn from areas we would not normally have had access to. She was also an excellent editor for style and consistency.

- **John Fauss and Gary Good, Amoco Production Company, Tulsa, OK**

    John is another new friend. He and his colleague, Gary Good, took the time to read and analyze our manuscript in record time. Their thoughts and comments were extremely helpful as we finalized the manuscript. Gary's background as the developer of the Text Display Facility, now marketed by VM/CMS Unlimited, Inc., gave us more insight into how others have solved the problems of displaying on-line text.

- **Elie Cassorla, Jim Slater, and their staff at the IBM Thomas J. Watson Research Laboratory, Hawthorne, NY**

    At the SHARE conference in August, 1987, Elie presented a session on SmartBook, a research project involving the use of on-line text display applications within IBM. Many of the ideas and presentation concepts were parallel to our ideas. He invited us to Hawthorne to discuss our ideas about on-line text, and to learn more about how the SmartBook design evolved.

We also owe a debt to our friends at QMS, Inc. in Mobile, Alabama, especially Diane Davis, Software Applications Engineer. The PostScript printer used for drafts and testing was their QMS PS/800+. Diane was often there to answer questions as we broke new ground by creating text and graphics on our mainframe and moved them down to the PostScript printer. Rick Gable at QMS was another source of help and encouragement as we came down to the final days of finishing the manuscript.

Phil Plumbo and Jewel Johnson at Printware, Inc. also provided attentive help when we reached the final challenge of making our host-produced PostScript actually print on a their PostScript printer.

Jeri Sampson, who was the Team Leader in DCF Development at IBM in Boulder, Colorado during much of the development of this book, was also extremely helpful as we installed the new version of the IBM Document Composition Facility which allowed us to produce PostScript from our mainframe. As with anything new, we had a few questions and opportunities, but Jeri was always able to help out, or get us to someone who could. Her friendship and help are appreciated.

We must also thank some of the people at Image Sciences, Inc.:

- **Michael D. Andereck, President**
  Michael allowed us the use of the time on the mainframe to develop the text and graphics for the book, which made drafting and revising the manuscript an easier task than it would have been if we had been confined to PC-based writing tools.

- **Garry Taylor**
  Garry is the MicroLab Project Leader on the Research and Design staff, and our resident superhero. Regardless of the problems we encountered as we tried new ways to create graphics on the mainframe for printing in the PostScript environment, or the opportunities presented when it came time to find a way to transfer our 85 MB PostScript file to the PC through software with a 64 MB transfer limit, Garry always had an idea and a solution. His friendship is highly valued, as is his ability to make just about anything work.

- **James Wirka**
  James is a technical writer in the Documentation department. As we came down to the final days, we used both his eyes and mind to make sure we were not missing obvious problems.

- **Stephen Poe**
  Stephen is the AI Project Leader on the R&D staff. He was a constant source of articles and books relating to human factors, text display, and just about any other topic we needed information about.

We also want to acknowledge the support of Jay Ranade, our series editor; Theron Shreve, our editor at McGraw-Hill; and especially Alan Rose of Intertext Publications. His patience and support as we introduced him to the concept of creating a document on the mainframe for printing on a PC-attached printer was admirable. We also appreciated his unwavering faith that we would come through.

And finally, we must thank our families for their support during the months of early mornings, late nights, and lost weekends it took to create this entity.

November, 1988

Part

1

Introduction

Before we launch into how to create a text retrieval and display system, we discuss the various types of on-line display applications, the questions surrounding how to provide some type of text examination on-line in a mainframe environment, and the reason you might want to attempt it. We also discuss why an on-line environment is desirable and the variety of situations which might change the way you would design such a system.

To help you understand the concepts associated with moving to an on-line documentation environment, we discuss the terminology associated with this type of text application.

We close with a description of the hardware and software required to provide up-to-date documentation and quality on-line help facilities to users of mainframe applications.

Chapter

1

What Is an On-line Text Access System?

A text access system is any type of on-line information system. It can refer to on-line help for a specific application, a computer-aided instruction course, or the software used to develop such a course. Or, it could be an on-line system for retrieval of the type of information traditionally found on paper, such as user manuals and reference documents.

In this book we strive to describe on-line text access without a bias toward any single need. We believe that, although the destination may vary, the path toward implementing any type of on-line text access system takes essentially the same direction.

Types of Text Access

On-line text access is the phrase we apply to the concepts involved in creating text files that can be accessed by a large number of end-users in the mainframe environment. It involves the creation of text files so that related information within any file can be found using well-defined structured search techniques and the further mapping to related information residing in other text files. It may also include the mapping of information to related application programs, or from related application programs, using an appropriate access method.

On-line text access does not stop with what is traditionally considered *on-line help*: the ability to access additional information from an application by pressing a function key. It goes a step beyond that concept to encompass on-line access to reference material and user documentation in a *free-standing environment*. And, finally, it includes *context-sensitive* entry into a text library.

We describe each of these aspects in much more detail in later chapters. Here we want to provide a high-level overview of these basic concepts as a foundation for our discussion of cost benefits and applicability. To help you to determine where on-line text display applications may fit into your business environment, review Figure 1-1. It highlights some of the more common business applications and the types of on-line display that are most useful for those applications.

On-line Help

Most mainframe environments include some type of on-line help system as part of the operating system and application software. For some systems and applications the help is extensive, including a panel that shows the syntax for commands, possible recoveries when errors are made, and examples of expected output. Sometimes large sections of the user and reference manuals are included. Most commonly this involves repainting the screen with the help information so that none of the application information is available to the user. An example of this type of help screen is shown in Figure 1-2 on page 6.

Alternatively, some systems are designed to permit the user to continue to see the application screen and display the help informa-

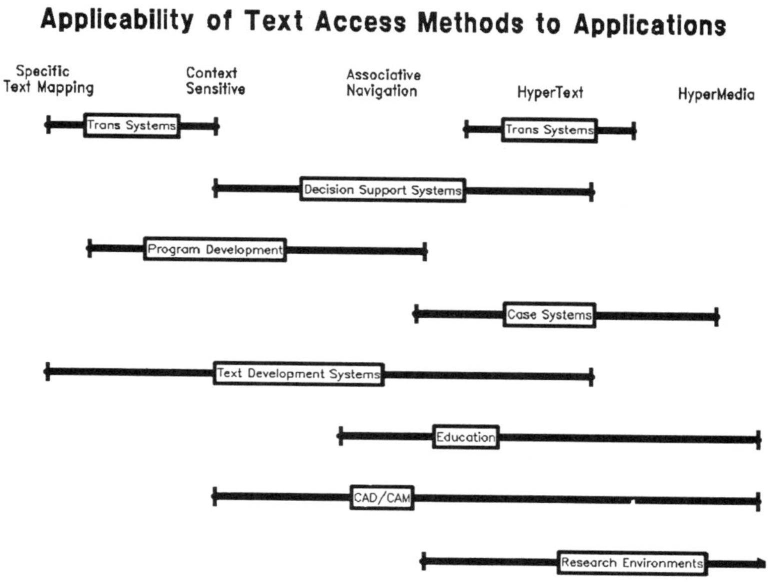

What Is an On-line Text Access System? 5

Applicability of Text Access Methods to Applications

Figure 1-1. Table of appropriate environments

tion in a window that overlays only a part of the screen image. An example of a window-based help screen is shown in Figure 1-3 on page 7.

Some systems are even sophisticated enough to allow users to determine the amount and type of help they need. In other systems the help is little more than a cursory overview of the syntax and valid values.

This type of help does not include intelligent determination of the type of help required, nor does it allow you to access the help system with natural language queries.

```
--> GSI DCF <=====> HELP   INFORMATION <=====>line ===> 1 of 223
The DCF EXEC

Use the DCF EXEC to execute IBM's Document Composition
Facility (DCF) and handle the output from it in a variety
of ways.  DCF EXEC can:

   - invoke a post-processor such as our DCF/PLUS
   - retain your options information, including fonts
   - retain your DCF output in a disk file
   - retain your output to your reader

DCF EXEC is a full-screen CMS/DMS application and can save your
screen variables in any user defined variable groups.  When
DCF is started, you have the opportunity to specify which
GROUP (or environment) you wish to have the screen restored
from.

The format of the DCF EXEC is:

---------------------------------------------------------------
|        | |                                                  |
|DCF     | | <font1 font2 ...> < ( <oldgroup> <newgroup> >    |
|        | -                                                  -
---------------------------------------------------------------
  1= All      2= Top      3= Quit    4= Return    5= Clocate     6= ?
  7= Backward 8= Forward  9= PFkey  10= Backward 1/2 11= Forward 1/2 12= Cursor

---->
                                                     Macro-read 1 File
```

Figure 1-2.   Example of full-screen on-line help

While a help system is the most common type of on-line text available to mainframe users, it does not have to be the only use of text access.

Free-standing Text Environments

Another common use of on-line text access is for simple information. A free-standing text environment might assume that the user is knowledgeable in how the files are arranged and named, or might have an application program running in front of it to aid in accessing the text. This type of system typically allows entry to an entire file, but does not provide references to other similar files or permit direct entry into a specific point in one or more text files related to a specific topic. Many public on-line databases and information retrieval services use this type of environment.

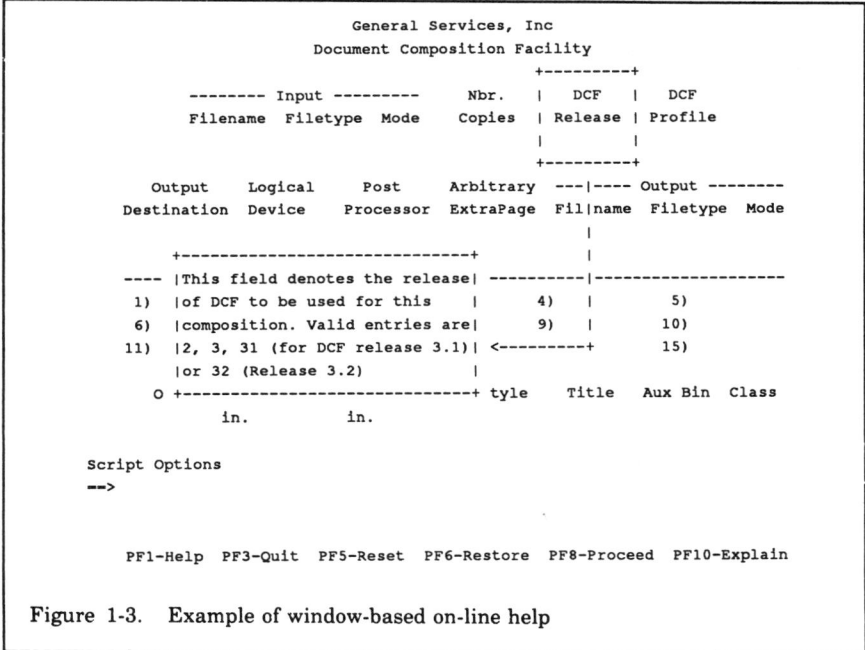

Figure 1-3. Example of window-based on-line help

Context-sensitive Text Environments

The most sophisticated on-line text access environment is one that knows what type of environment you are in and, at least in a rudimentary way, the type of information you require. Some are context-sensitive help systems that determine where you are in an application and the type of help you require to complete the task at hand.

Others are considered replacements for the volumes of user, reference, and other technical documentation an average user might need at hand in the performance of their normal duties. Some method of access is provided into the text library. That method provides a way to go directly to the pieces of text which are directly related to the current inquiry or to browse through a variety of files on a learning expedition.

Summary

Any of these methods provide some benefits to their user and to the user's management. The more sophisticated the on-line text access system, the more time must be spent on its design and implementation. However, a well-designed and integrated on-line text access system can provide great savings. We show how in the chapters to come.

Why Implement an On-line System?

Time and money are valuable resources to managers in any environment. Three of the most time-consuming problems faced by most managers are also costly problems:

- Educating every user about each on-line system

- Providing *everyone* with access to documentation

- Tracking available manual sets and their revisions

By providing instant access to correct information about any topic related to a worker's environment, on-line access to text can dramatically increase productivity. Everyone who has access to a terminal can have access to the text, although that access can be restricted as needed. Not only is the cost of creating/purchasing and distributing thousands of sheets of paper almost eliminated, but the security surrounding those documents can be enhanced. Paper documents can always be spirited off to a copy machine for reproduction; this can be much harder to do with a screen image.

In most shops a security system can be added to the text access system so that access to documents is permitted only to authorized readers. A sophisticated system can even produce reports to detail attempts at access by unauthorized users.

The question of updating documents held by the users is also eliminated. It becomes unnecessary to create, print, and distribute revisions, Technical News Letters (TNLs), or entire documents each time a change is made to the text. By maintaining the text in an on-line environment, changes can be entered, reviewed, approved, and made available in a fraction of the time required for the paper equivalent. This quicker access to the most recent information can eliminate countless problems, not to mention saving time and money. The requirement to notify users of changes to the files should not be ignored, though.

Depending on the size of your organization or client base, the cost of distributing updates to text maintained on paper can be enormous, discouraging the rapid deployment of new information. If you can eliminate or reduce these costs, however, the ability to update becomes a much less costly experience and permits more rapid dissemination of new information.

While the design and development of a comprehensive on-line text access system requires thought and a fair-sized budget, the benefits to any organization are immense. No MIS manager, or any other type of manager, should ignore the possibilities that the use of mainframe technology has to offer.

When Do You Need an On-line Application?

The area of on-line text access has the potential of being so broad that no one book can provide all of the information you might need. We did begin with a set of assumptions, however, that color how we approached on-line text in the manner presented in this book.

We believe that you must be interested in providing on-line access to some type of text perusal facility for the users of your application systems and that you want to provide this access in an IBM mainframe environment.

You may be a manager responsible for investigating the possibility of implementing such a system or a programmer interested in how such a system might be created. Your requirements might include the need to develop an on-line text access system in one or more of the following environments:

- In-house use with existing applications developed in-house
- In-house use with new applications developed in-house
- In-house use with purchased applications
- Sale to provide additional value to program products
- Sale to provide additional value to program products developed by other vendors

In all of these cases the approach to the creation and implementation of an on-line text display or on-line information system is quite similar.

We have tried not to assume any specific level of technical expertise in any of the areas related to on-line text access. While we have assumed you have a basic familiarity with the IBM/370 mainframe system and the applications running in your configuration of that environment, we do not assume much beyond that. For that reason, we discuss all of the technical terms associated with the many facets of on-line text access in *Caveats* on page 23.

Chapter

2

What Are the Benefits of an On-line System?

The decision to implement an on-line text access and management system requires serious consideration of all of the costs, the benefits they produce, and the changes in work patterns which ensue. Depending on the type of on-line system you envision, you may be able to work through the process slowly by implementing one level of access to on-line documents at a time. We recommended this approach.

But, before we delve into all of the possible implementation methods and the technical requirements behind the selection of the type of system to implement, carefully review each of the chapter topics. Since this is a fast-developing field, you should be prepared to evaluate the system constantly, or at least periodically, in light of new requirements and new technology.

Evaluating On-line Text

Something or someone sold you on the idea of investigating on-line text access systems for your business environment. Your next task is to define your environment and its needs well enough so that you can evaluate the effort required to implement an on-line text access and management system.

Your existing methods have the advantage of being in place and productive for you. You know what the fixed and fluctuating costs are, so budgeting is fairly easy from year to year. When it comes to documentation, the creation, printing, and distribution methods are probably known to most of your organization, and they may be quite comfortable with them.

Your existing methods, however, suffer several major drawbacks. The document creation process often requires the printing and distribution of paper copies of drafts. Each copy must be read and annotated, and then returned to the document originator. Then this process may be repeated a number of times, each requiring the printing of many draft copies.

When creation is complete and the final copy is ready, you may discover that thousands of sheets of paper have been spent in the process of creating those drafts, not to mention the man-hours consumed to print and distribute those drafts.

To further define the process you currently use, you must evaluate the following areas:

1. **Costs associated with keeping the existing methods for creating and disseminating information.**

    A major cost is in the time it takes to disseminate a change. It is not possible to keep up with every change in information and get it to every holder of a document in a timely and cost-efficient manner. When it does come time to make changes to documents, you must determine whether it is time to create and distribute entire documents to the entire user base, or to create and distribute update pages only. If you create and distribute only the updated pages, you place the burden of updating documents in the hands of the users, who often are too busy or just plain reluctant to manually insert the changed pages.

    This is a dangerous situation regardless of the type of document in question. How can you truly evaluate the cost in time

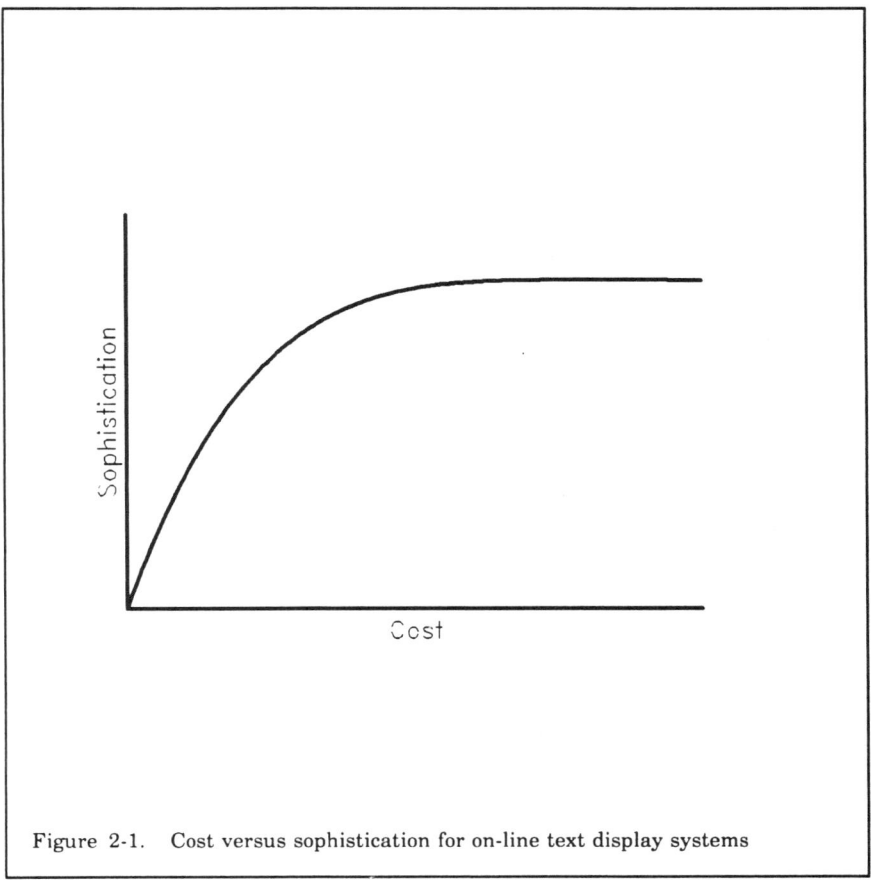

Figure 2-1. Cost versus sophistication for on-line text display systems

wasted, profit lost, or liabilities gained because an employee or customer used an out-of-date document to make a vital decision?

2. **Costs associated with implementing the system.**

Any change in methodology has costs associated with it. In this case the costs will fall into five areas:

- Hardware and software enhancements to accommodate the creation and viewing of documents on-line

- Preparation of existing text for inclusion in the on-line library

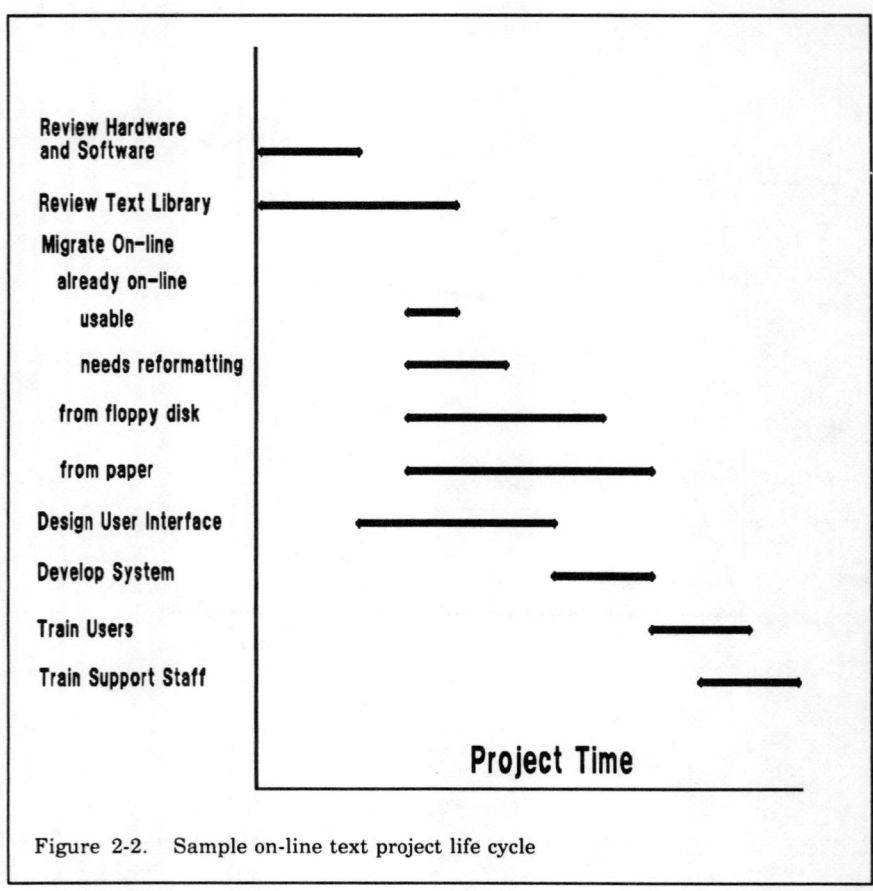

Figure 2-2. Sample on-line text project life cycle

- Retraining, either by vendors or an internal training group, to teach the on-line access methods and problem-reporting procedures

- Programming to create and integrate the system

- Support costs associated with both solving problems and enhancing the system over time

We discuss each of these areas in detail in later chapters. For the purposes of your initial evaluations, you must know the approximate costs associated with each item—based on the method of on-line text access and management you select. In *Evaluation Checklist* on page 99 we provide a source list for areas to review.

Figure 2-1 on page 13 illustrates a simplified view of the relationship between the cost of implementing an on-line text display system and the sophistication available for that cost. Guard against the tendency to believe that there is a one-to-one relationship between cost and sophistication. As shown by the curve, it is common to reach a point where the sophistication of the display system peaks regardless of the amount of money spent.

3. **Magnitude of the task to create an electronic library.**

   The transition to an on-line system is not a trivial one. If you already have most of your documents available in some type of electronic format, you are ahead of the game.

   If you have been having documents word processed or typeset or if you have a workstation or PC-based publishing system, you may be able to gain access to those diskettes or tapes and have them translated into a format compatible with the on-line system you design.

   The alternatives are to have the material re-keyed or scanned using Optical Character Recognition (OCR) scanners. Service bureaus are available in most cities to perform both services, although you may want to investigate the scanning alternative very carefully before making any decisions. The error rate for scanning material is often quite high. See *Scanners* on page 31 for more information on how this technology may fit into your solution package.

4. **Magnitude of the task to maintain an electronic library.**

   The creation of the electronic library is only the initial step in what becomes the maintenance cycle. There must be an ongoing and significant commitment to the process of keeping the electronic documents up-to-date, just as there has been for keeping the paper versions up-to-date. While the task does not change, you should find that how quickly that task is completed does change.

   You may also find that with an easier update methodology available there will be a tendency to reduce the amount of time between revisions. Allow for this in your planning to ensure that the proper procedures are in place to avoid unnecessary updates just because they are possible.

5. **Benefits of reducing or eliminating the creation and distribution of paper-based information.**

    By moving to an on-line environment for the dissemination of information, you can significantly reduce the costs associated with both the review cycle of a document and the updating of generally available documents. Not only is there a great savings in the staff associated with the development and approval process of a document, but also in the printing (in any form from photocopies to offset printing) and distribution. These costs vary from document to document within an environment, and from environment to environment, but they are always significant. Even if you do not eliminate the printing of documents entirely (which is usually an unrealistic goal), but you do reduce it by even half, the savings should be significant.

    The distribution area can present large savings because it is such a labor-intensive process. Look at how much of your yearly mail, internal and external, involves the distribution of documents and their updates. The savings are usually quite impressive, even in small companies.

6. **Benefits of providing accurate and up-to-date information on-line to the end-users of the system.**

    It is difficult enough to put a dollar amount on the benefits derived from knowing that your end-users have the most up-to-date and accurate information available with little effort on their part. Almost any dollar amount you derive will be a gross underestimation since you will also be reducing the liability associated with having incorrect information in the hands of your users.

7. **Quick response to problems found in documents.**

    In a traditional environment, it can be months between the time an inaccuracy is found in a document and the time that the correction is made and circulated. Many people never update their documents, which means that the incorrect piece of information is proliferated. Depending on the nature of the inaccuracy, this could make your business highly vulnerable to legal problems.

In an on-line environment, though, the inaccuracy can be noted and the proper group notified immediately. Major inaccuracies should be correctable within 24 hours, if not less.

8. **Quicker education for new employees.**
Often there is a lag time between when a new employee starts and when a complete desk set of manuals is made available. Or, worse yet, a new employee may either hear of a document they need or have to rely on sharing with another employee.

When you move to an on-line environment, all employees can have instant access to the on-line documents required for their duties.

This is also true when an employee transfers from one department to another. They can be locked out of the manuals they used to require and be given access to the manuals required for their new duties.

These initial considerations form the foundation. As you learn more about what types of systems can be created and evaluate which are most appropriate to your needs, there are more decisions to make.

Selling the Idea to Users

Do not forget that the goal is to have people using the system. You may meet some resistance as you try to sell the idea of moving to an on-line environment. These users may be comfortable with their dog-eared versions of manuals or may not have an affinity for terminals as a medium for information gathering. This is where your education process must begin.

Even if you sell your management on the cost justifications and benefits, if you cannot convince your users that the new system is an improvement and will make their lives easier, no amount of management support or coercion can make your implementation successful.

You may also encounter a group within your organization that wants to be on the leading edge. They want to find out what new technology in text access can do to make their environment more productive. You do not need to sell the idea to these people. In fact, your main challenge may be to help these people understand that you cannot throw away the existing system today and begin completely anew tomorrow. Change takes planning, management commitment, and time.

Sell your recalcitrant users with the following points:

1. **Ease of document creation and review.**

    Begin by selling document creators on how easy it is to create documents, circulate them for approval, and move them into production. As shown in Figure 2-3 on page 19, the document creation and distribution flow can be streamlined significantly by providing on-line access to document creators, reviewers, and users.

    Your text management system can include an annotation facility, which makes the review process for any document much easier. The document creator can look at each reviewer's comments, and the system may also be set up so that each reviewer can look at comments by other reviewers.

2. **Ease of access to up-to-date information.**

    Sell users on the fact that they will always have the most complete and current information available. The burden of keeping their manuals up-to-date is removed; they do not have to worry about adding new pages into their books. Nor will they ever again have to scout around for the latest copies of manuals which are not part of their desk set.

3. **Ability to maintain personal information within the document.**

    The system can also include a personal annotation facility to help the user add their own information to the on-line version of the document, just as they did with the paper copy. They do not lose the ability to "write in the margins" by moving to an on-line system.

4. **Elimination of mistakes caused by having the wrong information.**

    Remind the users that by having access to on-line information they should make fewer mistakes due to outdated data. This should be appealing to users who work in support situations and who are accountable for the information they pass to others.

5. **Addition of work space on the desk.**

    Most offices are not built for easy access to manuals while working. Using a manual often means laying it on the floor or

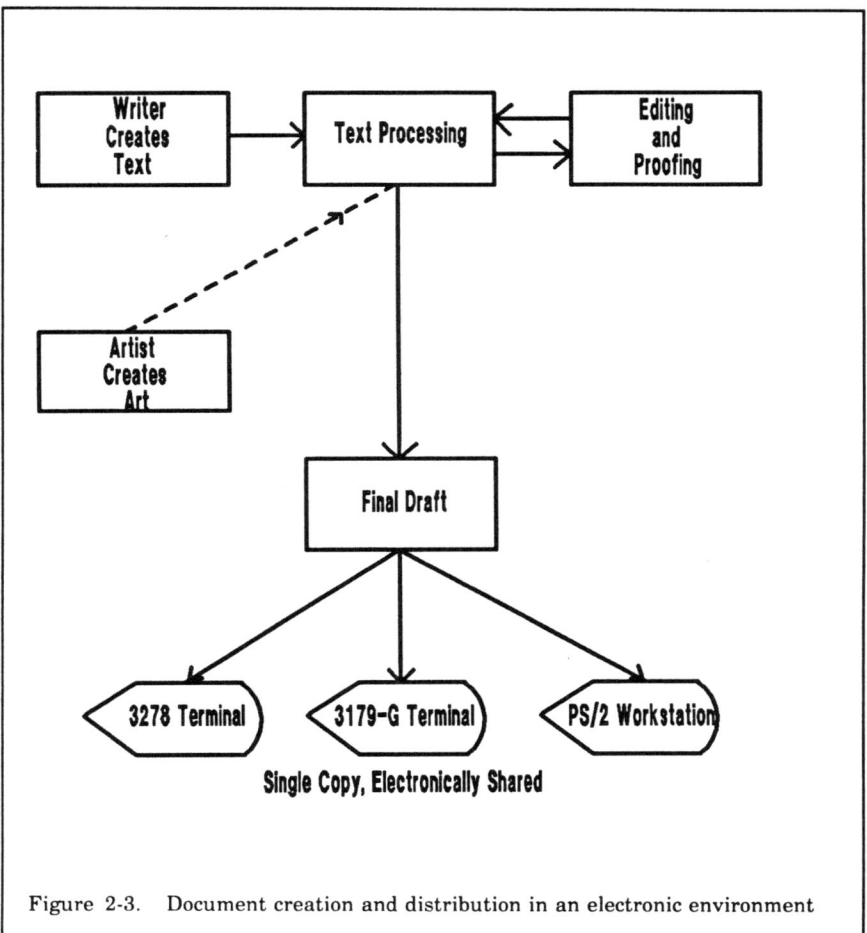

Figure 2-3. Document creation and distribution in an electronic environment

on top of other material. Even if you do have the desk space to keep one or two manuals open, each time another manual is needed you must shuffle things about. If update pages have not been incorporated, those take up space, too. With a move to an on-line text access system, this problem is eliminated.

The education process should begin early so that the users are brought into the planning process. Your user representative is your biggest sales aid, since that person knows the cost justifications, the hardware and software considerations, and the other advertised benefits of the system through the investigation process.

Additional Considerations

In the preceding sections we have alluded to a quicker turn-around time for revising documents. This should be a major selling point to both management and users. Depending on your type of production (traditional, demand printing, or on-line distribution), the benefits and the size of the selling job will differ.

In a traditional paper-based document environment, the document revision cycle may begin for any number of reasons. From the starting point the document may be marked up by a knowledgeable person, the changes keyed by a word processor or typesetter, and the entire document proofed by an editor. When the changes are complete, they may be sent to an art department to be added to the document masters on file. If documents are photocopied, that process is started. If documents are printed, then new negatives and plates are made for the appropriate pages.

If you are already in a demand publishing environment, you still must make changes, proof and validate them, and generate a new electronic copy to be made available for printing. The distribution may entail sending the entire document to all document holders, or revised page sets to some and entire documents only to new people.

In an on-line environment, if the commitment is made to update on-line documents at regular intervals, perhaps as often as weekly, you can reduce the legal exposure caused by inaccurate information in the hands of your users. There is no longer the major problem that the updates take too long to produce and distribute, nor is there the excuse for a user being uninformed because they did not receive an update. Everyone who has access to the system has access to the most up-to-date information.

Other selling points should include the enhanced security of information. It is much more difficult for an employee or guest to walk off with a complete document unless you give that person access to a printed copy or the ability to print a document from a terminal.

Caveats

While the creation and implementation of an on-line text display system can be a cost-effective solution to the problem of providing document access to the largest group of people, there are environments that may not be conducive to such a system. For example, if your environment is already suffering from an overuse of CPU resources, slow terminal response time, frequent turnover in technical support personnel, frequent turnover in systems support personnel, or a lack of on-site expertise in the implementation of large applications, you may find that an on-line text display system would make your environment less productive.

Chapter

3

Establishing a Baseline: Terms and Concepts

There are many new terms and concepts associated with on-line text which you will encounter as you explore this new technology. Some, such as *HyperText*, are strictly associated with on-line text, while others, like *DASD*, are more general computing terms. To ease you into these new terms, we have divided this chapter into the following categories:

- Storage Devices

- Other Hardware

- Software

- Organization of Information

Storage Devices

Computer *storage* is the medium for keeping electronic copies of your text and the programs that manipulate it. It is generally measured in millions of characters or *megabytes* (MB), but billions and even trillions of characters of storage are often discussed when talking about on-line text. The terms *gigabyte* (GB) and *terabyte* (TB) mean billions and trillions of characters, respectively.

To put this in perspective, consider that one megabyte is enough storage to hold about 200 double-spaced, typewritten pages. Therefore, one gigabyte is enough for about 200,000 such pages, and one terabyte of disk space can hold about 200,000,000 pages. Assuming two pages per sheet of paper (duplex printing), the stack of typing paper representing 200,000,000 pages would stand over 6 miles high—taller than Mount Everest.

Even the terms *millions*, *billions*, and *trillions* are not exact since computer storage is always measured in powers of two. The familiar *kilobyte* (KB) is 1,024 characters; a megabyte is 1,048,576 (1024 x 1024) bytes; a gigabyte is 1,073,741,824 (1024 x 1024 x 1024) bytes; and a terabyte is 1,099,511,627,776 (1024 x 1024 x 1024 x 1024) bytes.

So when we say that a terabyte of storage has a trillion characters, we have rather casually dismissed nearly 100 billion bytes. With a terabyte here and a terabyte there, we could be ignoring a great deal of memory.

Storage comes in three flavors in IBM mainframe:

- Virtual

- On-line

- Off-line

Virtual Storage

Most IBM mainframes have well under a gigabyte of real memory in the computer. In IBM operating systems, however, each user may have up to 2 gigabytes of *Virtual Storage* (VS). This 2 GB *address space* is memory that the operating system treats as an abstract entity rather than a real, physical quantity of memory built of integrated circuit chips. The concept of virtual storage is neither new nor simple, and is well beyond the scope of this book. However, the effect of VS is to provide the user the ability to run programs of immense size in much less real storage.

On-line Storage

On-line storage, also called *peripheral storage*, usually refers to storage on magnetic disk drives. Disks can hold many times the virtual storage capacity of a computer system, but the access to that data or text is slower than if the text is in virtual storage. Typical IBM disk drives, also known as *Direct Access Storage Devices* (DASD), have 2.52, 5.04, or 7.56 GB available for text storage.

DASD are typically magnetic in nature, storing data by recording information in a magnetic medium similar to audio tape, but with much lower error rates. In IBM host systems DASD are organized into *tracks*, concentric circles about the center hub of the disk, and *cylinders*, groups of contiguous tracks. At one time the term *cylinder* represented the physical vertical cylinders through disks which had multiple recording platters, but the one-to-one relationship of track to recording surface has gone by the wayside, leaving only the terminology behind.

Optical Storage Recently, a new technology has appeared which is quite applicable to on-line text storage. This is *optical disk* technology. Rather than storing data as magnetic recordings, optical disks record information as small holes burned into the surface of a plastic disk by a laser beam. Data is read back by bouncing a low-power laser off the *pits* (small pock marks in the disk) and the *lands* (the unburned areas between pits). As the reflection of the laser is distorted, digital information is recovered.

Optical disks are generally available in two formats and form factors:

- **Compact Disc-Read Only Memory (CD-ROM)**
  CD-ROM is virtually identical to the audio compact digital disc (CD) which has revolutionized audio playback in the past few years. A CD-ROM disk uses the familiar 4-3/4-inch diameter format. Most CD-ROM drives look like modified audio players; many are.

  CD-ROM cannot currently be recorded by the user, it is a read-only medium. It is suitable for the mass distribution of

reasonably static information such as reference materials. A CD-ROM holds approximately 600 MB of data.

- **Write Once, Read Many (WORM)**
  WORM disks can be written on once, can be read as many times as you like, but can never be erased and re-used. These disks come in either 5-1/4-inch or 12-inch platters and are usually packaged in a plastic cartridge which covers most of the disk. WORM disks hold up to 800 MB in the 5-1/4-inch form and up to 2 GB in the 12-inch form.

  WORM disks have an idiosyncrasy, however. Like most magnetic disks, they can be recorded on both sides of the platter. This is in contrast to the CD-ROM, which is only recorded on one side. WORM disk drives, however, have only read/write heads for reading one side. The WORM platter must be physically turned over to access all of its data. Devices to do this disk flipping have been developed.

  Such devices typically hold between 15 and 150 WORM disk cartridges and from 2 to 8 WORM drives. A robotic arm pulls a cartridge out of its storage slot, rotates it so that the correct side is facing the read/write head of the drives, then loads it into an empty drive. When necessary, the robot arm unloads one disk from a drive to flip it and reload it or to load a new disk. Such devices are called, appropriately enough, *jukeboxes*.

  An optical disk jukebox is exactly what it sounds like. It holds from 16 to 100 optical disks and 2 to 8 drives. When an optical disk storage program requests data on a particular disk, the jukebox moves a robot arm to a slot where the desired disk resides, extracts it, turns it over if necessary to orient the disk for accessing the desired data, then moves it to the designated drive. If necessary, the arm removes the disk currently in the selected drive and swaps it for the new one. The entire process takes about 15 seconds. The small, 16-disk jukebox can hold 32 GB of data while the larger, 100-disk jukebox can hold 200 GB.

Read/write optical disks are beginning to appear, but standards for recording methods and internal disk organization have not yet appeared. The price is still very high for read/write optical disk technology as well, but we expect that the price will drop considerably as soon as there are a few more vendors to choose from. The price per megabyte of optical disk storage is already better than magnetic, but few applications other than immense text storage have been found. Indeed, the CD-ROM industry is already questioning its long-term future since CD-ROM applications have not taken off as expected.

It is when you begin to examine the implications of optical disk that the need for such terms as terabyte appears. Consider that a single jukebox can hold up to 300 GB of optical disk storage. With only 4 jukeboxes you have 1200 GB, or 1.2 terabytes of on-line storage available. Optical technology will not soon supplant magnetic technology, however, because optical disks cannot be accessed and the data retrieved as quickly as magnetic disks can. Magnetic disk remains the choice for highest speed, but optical disk can easily coexist with magnetic disk to provide the highest storage capacity. Typically, for a given physical size disk, 5-1/4-inch or 12-inch, the optical storage capacity is 10 times that of the magnetic, but the access time for a random piece of text is also 10 times greater for optical disk than for magnetic.

Access time is the average time to access any piece of data on the disk. This means that the trade-off when using optical disk is between the vast amount of storage and the longer time to find a particular item stored. The cost per megabyte for optical disk storage is very low compared to magnetic disk, however, and the extra waiting time is insignificant in human terms. It can be up to 30 milliseconds for optical versus 3 milliseconds for magnetic media.

IBM does not currently support any optical disk system directly connected to any IBM host as a generally available product. IBM has provided mainframe optical disk connection for private contracts and it has announced an optical disk system which, through intermediate mid-range computers, can access optical disk systems. There are also several companies which have developed optical disk-to-mainframe links using personal computers and Local Area Networks (LANs) as links. See *Optical Disk Technology* on page 56 for a review of where this technology may fit into your environment.

Off-line Storage

Off-line storage usually refers to magnetic tape. IBM mainframes (also called *host systems* or *hosts*) use either model 3420 or model 3480 tape drives. Tape drives are considered off-line because the data on a tape cannot be automatically located and retrieved. To access tape-based data requires the intervention of a human operator to retrieve the tape and mount it on a tape drive. Magnetic tapes are terribly slow as compared to disk, but can hold vast quantities of data inexpensively. A *3420 tape reel*, which is the traditional 10-inch reel of half-inch computer tape, can hold several hundred megabytes for under $20. The newer *3480 tape cartridge* can hold several gigabytes of data.

You may encounter discussions of *optical tape*, which is beginning to make an appearance. This is plastic tape, similar to magnetic tape, but it is recorded using an optical technology similar to that used for WORM disks. Like WORM disks, optical tape can be written once by the user, then read as many times as needed. It has not made large inroads into the data storage product arena, but may become important as methods for connecting optical tape drives to host environments become available. There is, to our knowledge, no optical tape product which connects, even indirectly, to an IBM host system.

Before we close the discussion of storage terminology, there is one other term we must mention. There is a variation of off-line storage: *near-line storage*. This term is used to indicate that the data is not immediately available to a program, but can be automatically retrieved without human intervention. The optical disk jukebox is an example of near-line storage, as is the *Automated Tape Library* which is, essentially, a jukebox for the 3480 tape cartridges and drives.

It is sometimes hard to distinguish between on-line, near-line, and off-line storage systems. The important thing to remember is that they are best distinguished by the amount of time it takes to acquire information stored in any of the three methods. On-line storage can be retrieved in milliseconds, near-line in seconds, and off-line in minutes to days.

Other Hardware

We have already discussed much of the hardware in the previous section, but besides storage devices, there are many other pieces of equipment you must become aware of as you explore on-line text applications. This hardware includes:

- Terminals

- Displays

- Workstations

- Networks

- Scanners

Terminals

IBM terminals are of the *3270* family. These are the familiar green-on-black terminals seen in any IBM shop. They typically display 24 lines of 80-column text, no color and no graphics. The newer models are all 31xx terminals and take up much less space on a desk than the older 32xx models. The 3290 Plasma terminal permits up to four separate sessions on one terminal, all in 80-column mode.

There are some IBM 3270 terminals that display color and/or graphics. These are the 3179 and 3192 terminals. These terminals come in color only or color and graphics models. The 3179-G and 3192-G are the graphics versions.

Displays

We are separating displays from terminals because the display is so important to on-line text. IBM 3270 terminals are of relatively low resolution, even the graphics terminals which offer 768 x 384 *pixels* or dots on the screen. Typically, for good on-line *What You See Is What You Get* (WYSIWYG) graphics, you need at least 1024 x 1024 pixels–what is called a *megabit* or *megapixel* display. WYSIWYG technology is exactly what the acronym says—a display that precisely matches the image of a page as it would be printed on paper. The only IBM display which has such high resolution (and even a megabit display is considered medium resolution) is the 5080. This is not a terminal display you are likely to have in your office. It is a *Computer Aided Design* (CAD) terminal and is quite expensive.

The IBM 8514 monitor for the PS/2 has a resolution of 1024 x 768 pixels, which makes it the highest resolution PC monitor manufactured by IBM but puts it in the medium resolution group for WYSIWYG text. IBM also has a 19-inch monochrome monitor, the 8507, which offers the same resolution on the PS/2.

The resolution of the screen is important because it determines the quality and size of WYSIWYG text displays. Most desktop publishing systems utilize displays in 1280 x 960 resolution mode to view entire pages of text. IBM mainframe terminals, however, offer resolutions in the 768 X 384 range, which makes them unsuitable for true WYSIWYG text display of full pages.

Display resolution is one of the most important reasons why host-based on-line text access systems rarely employ WYSIWYG technology. The mainframe and 3270 terminal architectures are simply not designed for such *pixel-intensive* displays as the full pages of WYSIWYG text seen in many *desktop publishing* systems. Desktop publishing systems rely on the fact that there is a computer dedicated to each user, probably augmented with special display hardware, to display one or two pages of text in precise size, scale, and fonts. Mainframe users are constantly sharing the computer with other users, and there has not yet been sufficient computing power available to provide such support to mainframe users.

Workstations

There is a way to get high-resolution displays of WYSIWYG text from a host-based text access system: use personal computers as workstations.

Many companies have begun replacing their unintelligent 3270 terminals with personal computers, IBM PCs, PC *clones*, or IBM PS/2s. These personal systems are equipped with an adaptor and terminal emulator software that allows the personal computer to appear to be a 3270 terminal to the mainframe host (the mainframe CPU). This allows much of the workload of formatting high-resolution *bitmapped* displays to be offloaded from the host onto the PC or PS/2. Bitmapped displays allow every pixel or bit of the graphics and text on the screen to be separately controlled by the driving computer. To do this on the host requires expensive host CPU time (so-called *CPU cycles*), but a PC's CPU cycle is considerably cheaper. Also, since the PC is dedicated to one user, there is no contention for *CPU resources*.

Displaying bitmapped graphics on an IBM host is slow. Because of the terminal architecture, displaying large graphics such as bitmapped pages can also degrade other users' performance.

Networks

Many mainframe shops are beginning to connect their PCs together into *Local Area Networks* (LANs) which allow multiple PCs or PS/2s to share disk-resident data. These LANs are being connected to hosts through *gateways* which allow the host CPU to participate in the network as if it too were a PC. Such an architecture can be a major benefit to people implementing text access systems in a mainframe environment. LANs and LAN gateways allow high-resolution formatting to be performed by PCs serving as workstations, while accessing the vast quantities of text which can be stored and organized on the mainframe CPU.

Scanners

Acquiring text for an on-line text access system is a topic we devote much space to later in this book. *Optical scanners*, devices which digitally scan and store a document, are often considered to be the optimum text entry device. These devices can produce a bitmapped image of a document which can then be displayed on a workstation screen. Bitmapped images cannot, generally, be edited directly.

Some scanners can also perform *Optical Character Recognition* (OCR), where the bitmapped image of each character is examined, compared to patterns, and recognized for the letter it represents. Then, datastream in addition to a bitmapped image of the entire page, a datastream of the characters in each line is also returned by the scanner to the controlling computer. The datastream, rather than being a collection of black and white dots representing the image of the letters, contains one byte for each letter. Consequently, it is editable.

OCR scanners typically return datastreams in a format called *American Standard Code for Information Interchange* (ASCII), pronounced *ask-ee*. ASCII is the accepted code for PCs and most host computers in the world. IBM hosts, however, expect datastreams representing text to be coded in a format called *Extended Binary Coded Data Interchange Code* (EBCDIC), pronounced *eb-seh-dik*. Programs that transfer data from PCs or PS/2s to IBM mainframes translate the text from ASCII to EBCDIC.

Currently available OCR scanners are by no means 100% accurate in their interpretation of the actual character making up a line. Many scanners can only interpret typewriter-written documents, not typeset ones. Even for the most expensive scanners which can learn new fonts dynamically, an error rate of 3 letters out of every 100 is not uncommon. That translates to about 9 errors per typed page. The quality of the scan depends heavily on the quality of the input document, the contrast settings of the scanner, the intelligence of the software, and the amount of time the software can spend interpreting characters. A rate of several minutes per page may be necessary to scan and recognize even typeset documents with acceptable accuracy.

Software

As you investigate on-line text applications, you will encounter many software terms and descriptions which are not specifically concerned with text access. *Operating system*, for instance, is an important term to understand, but it is important to *any* computer system, not just text access systems. The operating system is the program which is initially loaded into the CPU, controls the execution of other programs, and provides management of such resources as disk and terminal access to those other programs. IBM mainframes typically run one of three major operating systems:

- Multiple Virtual Systems (MVS)
- Virtual Machine (VM)
- Virtual Storage Extensions (VSE)

This looks simple, but both MVS and VM come in several flavors:

- MVS/eXtended Architecture (MVS/XA)
- MVS/Extended Systems Architecture (MVS/ESA)
- VM/System Product (VM/SP)
- VM/eXtended Architecture-System Product (VM/XA-SP)

To add more complication, VSE is sometimes called the *Disk Operating System* (DOS) or DOS/VSE.

If you become involved in looking at a PC or PS/2 as the workstation for your text access system, you will encounter other operating system names. The three most popular operating systems for PCs or workstations are:

- Disk Operating System for PCs (MS-DOS or PC-DOS)
- Operating System/2 (OS/2)
- UNIX

Of these, MS-DOS and OS/2 are the most common within the IBM mainframe/PC world, while UNIX (or one of its variations, XENIX, AIX, SunOS) is popular with academics and workstation vendors.

Within the IBM mainframe arena there are a wide variety of software products, almost all represented by 3- or 4-letter acronyms. Gaining familiarity with these acronyms and the basic software concept each represents can help you avoid confusion as you navigate the IBM alphabet soup. We have organized these terms into a few categories to help you segregate them.

- Interactive Computing Environments

- Access Methods

- Composition and Printing

- Compilers and Subprograms

Interactive Computing Environments

The IBM operating systems described in the previous section provide only the ability to load and execute other programs. They do not offer facilities for performing *interactive computing*, which is the process of communicating with programs through a terminal. For on-line text access, there must be an on-line, interactive computing environment. IBM supplies many of these, sometimes several for a given operating system. The one you use to support your on-line text facility depends on which operating system you have and what your corporate needs and requirements are.

For MVS In MVS there are several interactive computing environments. The most common is the *Time Sharing Option* (TSO). TSO provides the program execution facilities of MVS to users logged onto a terminal. The *CLIST* language provides the ability to build TSO command streams that execute programs one after another, automatically. This facility is called a *command language*. Most interactive computing environments offer one. An optional product to improve TSO's usability is the *Interactive System Productivity Facility* (ISPF). ISPF provides facilities for designing and managing *dialogs* that display full screen *panels* of text. ISPF can be augmented by another package, the *Program Development Facility* (PDF), which provides such utilities as a *full-screen editor* to help programmers and text writers produce the programs and documents they need.

Other interactive computing environments in MVS include the *Customer Information Control System* (CICS) or the *Information Management System* (IMS), but such productivity features as editors and dialog managers may have to be purchased from third party vendors or implemented by your company's programming staff.

For VM VM systems come with the *Conversational Monitor System* (CMS), which provides a full range of interactive computing facilities including the *XEDIT* full-screen editor. XEDIT can also be used to develop full-screen panels for the display of text. CMS offers 3 command languages, the most powerful is the *Restructured Executive Executor* (REXX) language.

For VSE VSE users must install CICS in order to gain an interactive computing facility. Under CICS they can install IBM's *Interactive Computing and Control Facility* (ICCF), which includes a full-screen editor and program execution facilities. It does not, however, provide a command language.

Access Methods

Access methods are programs which are part of the operating system, but which application programs, such as an on-line text access system, use to manage data and information on disk, tape, print, and terminals. Each of the several IBM access methods has a four-letter acronym which ends in *AM*, standing for *access method*.

Two of the major access methods have very similar acronyms: VSAM and VTAM. The *Virtual Storage Access Method* (VSAM) is a method of organizing data on DASD. VSAM supports several different organizations of data, which are discussed in *Data Organization* on page 41. The *Virtual Telecommunications Access Method* (VTAM) is the latest IBM product for managing communications to terminals and other computers. It is part of IBM's *Systems Network Architecture* (SNA), which is a set of *protocols* for device-to-device communication.

VSAM replaced older access methods for disk data, which you may still encounter.

Composition and Printing

IBM host-based text composition is typically accomplished using a batch text processor. The term *batch* refers to the fact that the program does not directly interact with a terminal and user; instead it reads input from a disk file, processes it, then writes output to a disk file. The three text composition systems most widely used in the IBM world are IBM's *Document Composition Facility* (DCF), the *Xerox Integrated Composition System* (XICS) and Applied Data Research's *Extended Text Composition Facility* (ETC).

Document Composition Facility (DCF) DCF is a host-based batch composition product that produces both simple composed text for line printers using *fixed-pitch* fonts (each character has the same width and height) and composed text in a format known as the *Advanced Function Printing Data Stream* (AFPDS) for the IBM AFP printer family. AFPDS fully describes each page as a hierarchically organized set of *structured fields*. This permits AFP printers such as the IBM 3820 and 3827 to print text in *proportional fonts* (each character has its own width, which improves readability).

When you produce printed output the question of whether to use fixed-pitch or proportional type is usually answered on the side of using proportional type. It is typically much easier to read proportional type, and it presents a much more professional image. When you move into on-line display, however, the question of type display is often a question of what type of display system you can afford, and the type of character display it uses. Most commonly used terminals are limited to fixed-pitch character display on the terminal, although some of the high resolution displays can support the use of proportional fonts. For most display applications the use of proportional fonts is not required. In fact, some people find that proportional fonts become harder to read after spending long hours viewing text on a terminal.

DCF can also produce PostScript output. PostScript is a *page description language* supported for many desktop printers. It is also supported by several typesetting systems because PostScript output is *device independent*. This means that the datastream does not need to adapt or change for devices with higher or lower *resolution*—the number of dots per inch printed by the printer. Font scaling within the PostScript interpreter accommodates the various resolutions found among PostScript printers. The PostScript interpreter program resides within the printer. Another advantage to

PostScript is the availability of the PostScript Display program for routing output to graphics terminals for softcopy preview.

Advanced Function Printing Products IBM has created an alphabet soup of programs and acronyms associated with Advanced Function Printing (AFP). Although these AFP products are not particularly important to on-line text systems, you should be aware of them so that you do not get confused when you encounter them. They include:

- **Overlay Generation Language (OGL).** The OGL language is used to design electronic forms as text overlays.

- **Page Printer Formatting Aid (PPFA).** PPFA is used in batch environments to create page printing resource objects called *pagedefs* and *formdefs*. Pagedefs control the layout of logical pages for AFP printers. Formdefs control the printing of the physical page.

- **Print Management Facility (PMF).** PMF is used in both batch and interactive environments to create pagedefs and formdefs, to create and modify fonts for use on AFP printers, and to modify *page segments*. Page segments are objects that can contain composed text and graphics. They are created and formatted independent of the text and included in the document using a callout to the object name.

- **Font Library Service Facility (FLSF).** FLSF provides font editing and management facilities in a batch environment.

Other Interfaces When DCF is the composition system of choice, but the printers of choice are non-IBM printers, you normally need some type of interfacing software to transform the AFPDS output into a form compatible with the target printer. Several products, such as Image Sciences, Inc.'s DCF/PLUS, can take AFPDS and transform it into metacode for printing on the Xerox Centralized Laser Printers, *QUIC* for printers by QMS, Inc., or *UDK* for Xerox Decentralized Laser Printers, such as the Xerox *3700*, and *4045*, and Diconix *Dijit 1*.

Xerox Integrated Composition System (XICS) XICS is a host-based batch composition product that can produce output compatible with many typesetting systems or Xerox Metacode, a datastream native to the large Xerox laser printers, such as the *9790*, the *8790*, or the *4050*. A metacode datastream can include callouts to fonts and graphics which makes it possible to produce printed output of near typeset quality.

XICS code can also be produced by several workstation-based products marketed by Xerox.

Host Forms Description Language (HFDL) HFDL is a Xerox forms design language which runs on the IBM host. It is a batch composition product that allows you to design electronic forms for Xerox Metacode printers in the same type of structure that OGL provides for IBM AFP printing environments.

Extended Text Composition (ETC) ETC is a host-based composition language that is marketed by Applied Data Research for use in environments which use their Remote OS Conversational Operating Environment (ROSCOE) product. It produces output in line printer format which can be sent to any print device that looks like a standard IBM line printer device. Because ETC output is in line printer format, it would be quite easy to manipulate its formatted output for display to the screen in a user-friendly manner.

Compilers and Subprograms

There are a variety of *compilers* in which your text access system may be written. These are the programming languages used by IBM users and software vendors to implement computer systems. The languages currently in use in many IBM shops include:

- **Assembler Language Code (ALC).** ALC, sometimes referred to as BAL, is a language in which each instruction translates directly into a machine instruction. While this allows powerful access to machine functions and can result in the most efficient programs, ALC is time consuming and difficult to program. The detail required for ALC programming does not lend itself to text applications, but it can occasionally be useful for writing input/output (I/O) routines.

- **Common Business Oriented Language (COBOL).** COBOL is a popular business language, but it is not well suited to text manipulation and management.

- **Programming Language/1 (PL/1).** PL/1, sometimes listed as PL/I, is a very powerful language that is particularly well suited to text access and graphics programming.

- **Formula Translator (FORTRAN).** FORTRAN is an old language, primarily used for mathematics and engineering. It is a poor choice for text and is being supplanted by PL/I for graphics.

- **PASCAL.** This language is similar to PL/I and popular among PC users, but seldom used by mainframe programmers. For text applications it does offer many built-in functions.

- **C.** C is new to mainframe programming, but very popular with PC programmers.

- **A Programming Language (APL).** APL is an *interpreted* language, meaning it is not compiled all the way to the native machine code. Consequently, it runs a bit slower than the compiled languages listed above. APL handles arrays of numbers very efficiently, but programs written in APL can be very difficult to understand and maintain. IBM's PMF is written in APL, but this is rare among text applications.

- **Restructured Executive Executor (REXX).** REXX is also an interpreted language currently available only to VM and PC users, although we expect it to become available to MVS users soon. REXX is very much like PL/I in structure and syntax and is an excellent text manipulation language. It is slower than compiled languages due to its interpreted nature, but does make an excellent prototyping language.

COBOL, FORTRAN, C and REXX have been designated as part of IBM's new *Systems Application Architecture* (SAA), a collection of standards for the design, look, and feel of future software products to be available across IBM's computer processing lines. You may want to look at developing an in-house text access system in one of these languages to maintain compatibility with trends in IBM programming. Of these languages, we recommend REXX for prototyping and C for final coding. Although PL/I is probably the best compiled language for final code instantiation.

Aside from compilers or interpreters, there are also subprogram systems that are used to write programs. It is important to understand the role of such subprogram systems. They are **not** program systems themselves. That is, you do not execute one of these programs to achieve final output. They are programmers' tools which would otherwise have to be written by each shop. The *Graphical Data Display Manager* (GDDM) is one of the most common sets of subprograms. GDDM is a set of subprograms which provide graphics support to IBM terminals and printers. GDDM consists of several hundred individual subprograms and a variety of utility programs which are, themselves, GDDM applications.

You can also acquire the *Presentation Graphics Feature* (PGF), which is a set of GDDM application programs designed to help construct business graphics. PGF includes the *Interactive Chart Utility* (ICU), which is an interactive application for designing and viewing business charts and graphs.

VSAM, VTAM, and the other access methods are also subprogram systems that your programming staff calls from application programs to accomplish data management. VSAM and VTAM come with utility programs that are applications of the access methods.

Database management systems, such as *DataBase 2* (DB2) or *Structured Query Language/Data System* (SQL/DS) or *Data Language 1* (DL1) typically consist of subprogram sets that your application programmers must call from the programs they write to invoke the database management services. Database management systems also have utility programs which are included or which can be purchased separately. The utilities are applications of the subprogram systems. One example is *Query Management Facility* (QMF).

A final set of subprograms you may hear about are the *Library Management* (LM) routines of PDF. These routines allow you to store data in IBM libraries under MVS.

Organization of Information

We are grouping several terms under the heading of organization of information, because they deal with how to think about organizing information and resources. These terms may be related to:

- Document Organization

- Data Organization

- System Organization

Document Organization

While paper documents are typically organized in a linear fashion, on-line documents can be organized in a multitude of ways. The term *linear document* refers to documents which are meant to be read from the first page to the last. An example of such would be a list of assembly instructions for a machine part. *Non-linear documents* are organized in such a way that the reader must, or is at least encouraged to, skip around from topic to topic and page to page, not following any obvious sequence. Programmed instruction manuals are examples of such non-linear document organization.

Non-linear documents can be organized as a *hierarchy*, in which each small topic leads to larger ones; a table of contents is an example of this. They may also be organized as a *network*, in which topics randomly suggest other topics that may or may not be at a greater level of detail. Encyclopedia articles and bibliography entries are examples of such networked documentation.

The term *HyperText* refers, in general, to non-linear documents, but more specifically to computerized systems of documentation that support and utilize non-linear documents. HyperText systems and the *HyperDocuments* stored within them are usually a mixture of hierarchical and networked structures. Such traditional hierarchies as tables of contents continue to exist in HyperDocuments, but they are augmented by the presence of *HyperText links*, which interconnect document elements in a networked fashion.

HyperText links exist between *HyperText nodes*—the actual pieces of text connected together by the links. The software that manages and navigates the HyperDocument uses the links to do so. Typically, links have semantic information associated with them, such as *link names* or *link types*.

In addition to the hierarchical and networked document structures present in HyperText systems, the documents can also be considered to be *associatively* structured. By this we mean that searches and connections can be made by the reader, who uses generic keys that the system either finds in the current and other documents or treats as synonyms for information in those documents. Typically, once an associative link is established, the HyperText user can create a standard HyperText link to preserve the context and results of the associative structure.

One step beyond HyperText systems are *HyperMedia* systems, which use the HyperText concept of links and nodes to access non-textual material. HyperMedia systems combine standard text and graphics with animated graphics, video, and/or audio. All of this is organized so that the user may not even be aware of the nature of the medium of the next accessed node. A request to follow a link from a piece of text may land the user in a pre-recorded lecture on the topic by a famous professor, or it may cause a rotating, three-dimensional drawing of the object under discussion to appear.

Data Organization

A separate issue from how text documents are semantically organized is that of how the text is organized as data within the on-line access system. The data organization strategy is very important to the performance of the system. Forcing certain functions on the wrong data organization can slow a function-rich system to a crawl.

Within traditional IBM mainframe architectures there are a limited number of ways data can be organized. IBM access methods are all *record oriented*, meaning that a collection of related fields is organized into a linear strip called a *record*. Related records are collected into a *file*. A file may contain records which are all of the same length, that is the record length is *fixed*, or the record lengths may be *variable* up to some limit. Fixed-length files are a bit faster to access and scan, but variable-length record files are more conserving of space.

For MVS and VSE

There are several ways in which files can be organized for access. These are all represented within VSAM, and therefore, we will concentrate on its terminology. Other access methods use the same organizational structures with some jargon differences. VSAM is widely used in MVS and VSE environments, much less so in VM systems. VSAM supports 3 types of files:

- Entry Sequenced Data Sets (ESDS)
- Key Sequenced Data Sets (KSDS)
- Relative Record Data Sets (RRDS)

An ESDS is the simplest form of file. Records are accessible in the sequence in which they were entered. They may be either fixed or variable. There is no higher-level indexing structure on top of an ESDS for an application program to use when retrieving information.

KSDS is probably the most common VSAM file organization. A KSDS has an index file associated with it. The index contains information for finding records in the main file directly, without searching the entire file. The index is built from keys which are part of the main file. Only a small part of each record is designated as a key and it must be a set of contiguous columns in the record.

It is possible to define *alternate indexes* over a KSDS that have other keys specified. The data can be accessed through a *path* that specifies which alternate index to search through. The two drawbacks to this scheme are:

- Multiple alternate indexes require a lot of space.
- When a record is changed, all of the indexes must be updated to retain total integrity. This can pose a large overhead on the CPU.

The RRDS organization is seldom used, but has a lot of advantages in certain applications. RRDS files must have fixed-length records. The records are retrieved by specifying a relative record number: record 1, record 5, record 3243, and so on. Direct access is easily achieved, but the application must have some way of determining which record is desired.

MVS supports both the VSAM file organization and a non-VSAM file organization, called the *Partitioned Data Set* (PDS). A PDS is well suited for storing many small files, called *members*, in a single file where they can be easily accessed by an 8-character name. Program *libraries* and many other sorts of libraries are used by the operating system, TSO, and other applications. A PDS is probably the most obvious choice for storing text since each separate document can be given a name.

For VM VM/CMS uses an altogether different file system, one which automatically provides ESDS and RRDS types of access for both fixed- and variable-length record files. There is no native CMS facility comparable to KSDS; the user must use VSAM for keyed access. PDS organization is supported, but not well enough to make it popular.

CMS systems give each user a *minidisk*, which appears to the user to be a complete but small disk. In actuality it is a piece of disk space essentially carved out of the middle of a big disk. A minidisk can be any size up to the full size of a disk, but is usually only a few cylinders. CMS uses a file naming scheme involving 8-character *filenames* and 8-character *filetypes*. The concept of a library can be implemented by designating an entire minidisk to be a library or by designating that all files with a given filetype constitute a library.

Libraries, particularly for text documents, can be built on RRDS files by the use of *linked lists*. A linked list is a set of records linked together by each record containing the relative record number of the next record for that particular list. For instance, a text member in such a library might consist of record 5 which points to record 7 as the second element of the list. Record 7 might point to record 3 as the third element. In some linked-list structures each record points back to the previous record in the list as well as forward. Such a linked list is said to be *doubly linked*. The *head* and *tail* of the list, the first and last records, are identified by zero backward and forward pointers, respectively.

Linked list organizations are particularly well suited to text storage systems because they are very efficient and easy to program. They are, however, difficult to search.

Database Organization

Database management systems build on these traditional organizations, offering significantly more flexibility and functionality in searching and retrieving data. The two most common database organizations are:

- Hierarchical
- Relational

We also look at content-based database organization, a relative newcomer to database organization technology.

IMS is the most familiar hierarchical database on IBM mainframes. These databases are organized as an inverted tree structure where there is a high-level object that points to lower-level *children*. Each of these may, in turn, point to children of their own.

Hierarchical organization is quite natural to text access systems since documents are often stored hierarchically.

> Books have sections,
> which have chapters,
> which have subchapters,
> which have paragraphs,

which have sentences,
which have words,
which have letters.

IMS, unfortunately, is rather expensive to acquire, difficult to program, and cumbersome to run. These factors have led to other, home-grown hierarchical systems being developed for text.

Relational database organization has become the dominant database technology in the last decade. IBM's mainframe relational products are DB2 in MVS and SQL/DS in VM. Both of these use *Structured Query Language* (SQL) as the database interface language.

Relational databases are collections of *tables*. Each table consists of *rows* and *columns*. Roughly speaking, tables correspond to files, rows to records, and columns to fields within records. Relational functions allow data from the tables to be mixed and matched in complex and highly versatile ways. In a language like SQL, it is possible to state a query such as,

> *Retrieve the activity number, date, and abstract from the activity table and the associated customer name and address from the client table where the activity is less than 30 days old, the client is from the northeast, and the activity is against only the product ABC.*

The relational database system performs all the necessary matching and combining of tables to produce a *virtual* table whose rows contain the requested columns and whose data matches the specified criteria.

The term *virtual* refers to the fact that a computer-based object, such as a relational table, a peripheral device, or even storage, may exist only as an abstract construct within the machine. A virtual table is one which is created from the logical joining of real tables, but which never actually exists in the database. It only seems to.

Using this concept, operating systems may allow programs to execute with much more *virtual storage* than is actually present in the real machine. Indeed, in IBM's Virtual Machine operating system, whole CPUs are simulated as *virtual* machines. Each user *appears* to have a complete computer complex, but is actually sharing a single real computer system.

Relational databases are not specifically designed to search long, free-form text documents, however. They are geared toward the search of well-defined columnar data, and their power is best seen when they are matching fixed-length numeric data. Free-form, flowing text, where the desired information might appear anywhere in a record, or even span multiple records, is not the sort of information that relational databases were designed for. Nonetheless, they are in fairly wide use for text storage and retrieval systems and can be coerced into supporting many desirable text retrieval functions. In particular, well-formed information about the text, so called *meta-knowledge*, can be effectively stored in relational databases.

Perhaps the most sophisticated and appropriate text storage organization technology is that of *content-based* access. In a content-based *textbase* every significant string of text is indexed and available for use during search and retrieval operations. Documents can be organized hierarchically or in a networked fashion more suitable to HyperText systems. Multiple documents can reside in a single physical file, each document can be in a separate file, or the system may use a combination.

Systems which use content-based organization are rare on IBM mainframes and, except for IBM's *VM Contextual File Search* (VM/CFS), are available only from third-party vendors. These systems use sophisticated hashing algorithms and synonym dictionaries to search and locate text elements with much more speed and versatility than any of the organizations described above. They also, typically, use a minimum of space for their indexes and do not require a lot of file preparation before they can be applied. The existing text, be it in composition source code form or in composed, print-ready form, can be indexed without having to be migrated into a different data organization.

System Organization

Any interactive system has its own internal organization which the user must learn to navigate to use the system. On-line text access systems are no different. The system you are implementing or evaluating may be *command-driven*, *menu-driven*, *windowed*, or some combination of these.

Command-driven systems have a command line on virtually every screen in the system. There should be a list of commands available, and you should be able to access help information on any command from any screen in the system. Most command-driven systems do not offer any display that indicates overall system organization because there is none. All commands are usually valid from any screen with no way to predict where a user is going next.

Menu-driven systems offer panels of selections, as in a restaurant menu. Ordinarily there is a selection field into which you can type the number or letter of the menu item desired from that screen. Some screens may use function keys to indicate selections or may ask you to position the cursor at an item, then press a key to indicate an action. Menu-driven systems are well organized; many are able to display the hierarchical structure of the menus either on the screen or in the printed documentation. This can be an invaluable aid for navigating the system. Usually, the final menu selection on any branch in such a system causes a panel to be displayed that has no further menu items; it is either a display-only panel or a data-entry panel.

Windowed systems partition information into small, rectangular areas on the screen. These areas are called *windows* because they act as a window into the system. The windows may be overlapping, in which case the most current, active window is the one that is not overlaid by any other. If the windows are never allowed to overlap, the system is said to use *tiled* windows because the windows are placed on the screen like tiles on a wall.

Windowed systems may allow the windows to be dynamically moved or re-sized while you are viewing them. They may also offer menu selections in *pop-up* or *pull-down* menus. Pop-up menus usually appear in the middle of the screen whenever needed and disappear when a selection is made. Pull-down menus generally hang from a *menu bar* (positioned along the top or side of the screen). Pull-down menus seem to drop down from the menu bar and then close up into it again like a window shade.

Some windowed systems offer *scroll bars* to help you perform horizontal and vertical scrolling. These are lines at the bottom and along one side of the screen that indicate where you are positioned in the text you are viewing. By placing the cursor in a scroll bar and pressing a key, you cause the window to be moved to a different place in the overall document.

Many windowed text access systems, particularly HyperText systems implemented in a windowed manner, offer *browsers*. These are displays of the connected structure of documents and windows within the system, sometimes in graphic format and sometimes in nested list format. These are useful while learning the system, but you may not want them to intrude into day-to-day usage since many users find them annoying. If one is provided, it should be optional.

Window systems are just becoming available on mainframes. Traditionally, window environments on PCs require graphics and *live keyboards* (where the CPU is aware of every keystroke), not just program function (PF) and **ENTER** keys. Because IBM mainframe terminals are not architected this way, windowed systems are only now beginning to catch on. Most host-based text access systems are menu-based with some command-driven capability. TSO's ISPF is an example of a mixed Command/Menu system.

Chapter

4

Minimum Mainframe Requirements

What is required in the way of mainframe hardware and software to support an on-line text system? We have been presuming that you intend to implement this system in an IBM 370 mainframe environment that includes some combination of the following hardware and software:

- **A System 370 or 370/eXtended Architecture (XA) CPU.**
  This may be an IBM computer or a *plug-compatible* computer from a third-party vendor, such as Amdahl.

- **A System 370 operating system from IBM:**

  ° MVS/ESA
  ° MVS/XA
  ° VM/XA
  ° VM/SP
  ° VSE

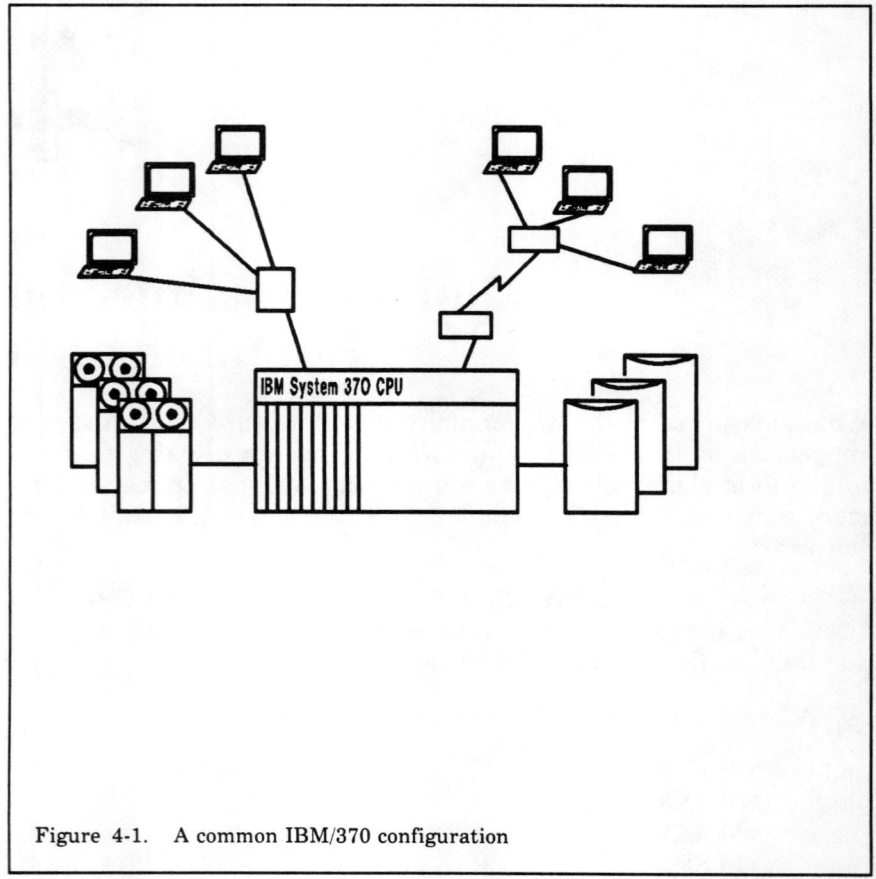

Figure 4-1. A common IBM/370 configuration

- **An interactive computing component for your operating system such as:**

  ◦ CICS
  ◦ IMS
  ◦ TSO
  ◦ CMS
  ◦ ICCF

- A full-screen text editor running under the interactive computing component such as:
  - CMS/XEDIT
  - TSO/PDF Editor
  - A third-party editor
  - VSSE/ICCF Editor

- A network of 3270 architecture terminals or personal computers serving as terminal workstations.
  These may consist of such terminals as:
  - PS/2 with the Graphics Workstation Program
  - PC/AT-GX with the Graphics Control Program
  - 3192-G Distributed Function Terminal
  - 3179-G Distributed Function Terminal
  - 3192-3 Text-only Terminals
  - 3178-2 Text-only Terminals
  - PS/2 with the 3270 Emulator Program
  - PC/AT or PC/XT with the 3270 Emulator Program

- **At least a gigabyte of on-line disk storage**
  Use Figure 4-2 on page 52 to help define your choices for storage media.

Your system may consist of any combination of these hardware and software components. The sophistication available for your on-line text system is largely dependent on what combination of these components you use to implement it. To get the most sophisticated system, you will require other hardware and software not listed above. To get a good entry-level on-line text system you only need a subset of what's listed above. You should, however, be prepared to upgrade some hardware and software to implement the on-line text access facility that you choose.

CPU Power

On-line text access can swallow a lot of CPU resources, but this does not have to be so. If your text is pre-formatted for display prior to retrieval, much of the CPU overhead associated with text access can be reduced to creation and maintenance formatting tasks. It does not require much CPU to retrieve and display a piece of formatted text, but the process of composing and setting the text is computer

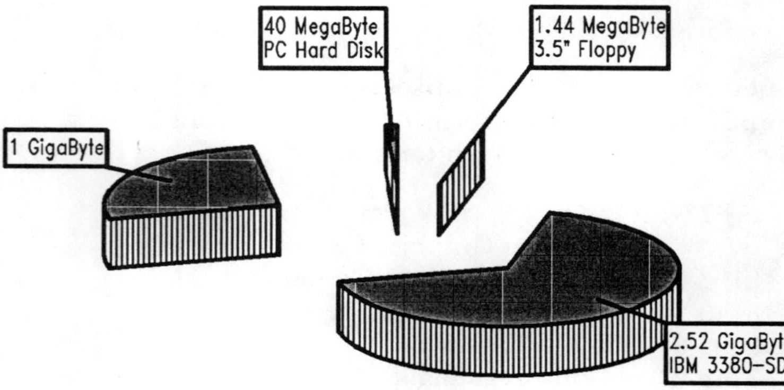

Figure 4-2. Relationships between various storage media

intensive and can degrade performance for everyone on the system, not just the text user.

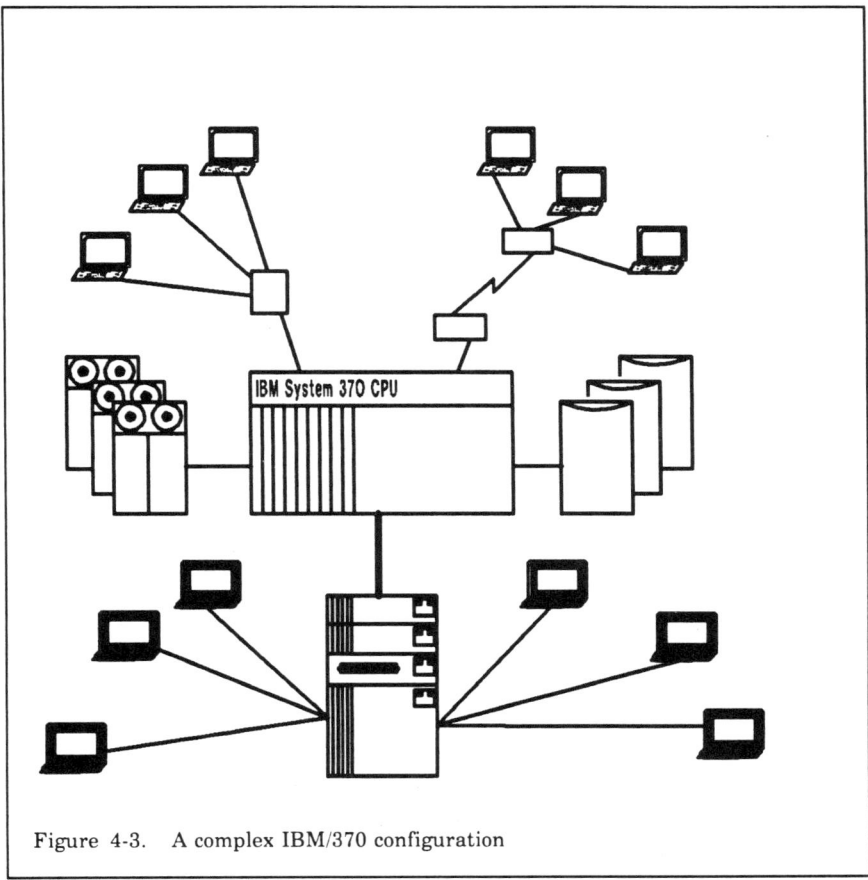

Figure 4-3. A complex IBM/370 configuration

We discuss this consideration in more detail later, but you should give serious consideration to maintaining sub-second response for on-line text users. This may entail a separate CPU on which the retrieval process executes. The IBM 9370 is a small, relatively inexpensive processor that can be connected to a larger CPU and used exclusively for providing the on-line text processing power necessary to provide sub-second response. The IBM 43xx family of processors is also a good candidate for this job. Figure 4-3 illustrates a sample configuration using this idea.

Retrieval software, with its elaborate indexing requirements, can be CPU intensive as well, particularly if indexes are retained in virtual storage to reduce device I/O activity. Carefully evaluate the retrieval systems and their CPU requirements. The relational database type of retrieval system described in *Database Organization* on page 43 make serious computing demands on the CPU, while more sophisticated content-based access methods do not impose nearly as high a CPU overhead.

Retrieval is always a trade-off between CPU and I/O device activity. I/O activity always takes longer and is generally reduced by maintaining more data in virtual storage, but this can cause such computer intensive operations that other users do not get a fair share of the CPU. Tuning your text access system to even out this mix of CPU activity and I/O activity is one of the most important tasks during the implementation and testing of a finished text access system.

Storage Requirements

Text access systems may require several types of storage:

- Virtual Storage
- On-line Storage
- Near-line Storage
- Off-line Storage

Virtual Storage

Virtual storage is the computer memory used during actual execution of the system. As stated above, many text access methods use a lot of virtual storage to reduce the need to issue reads to disk devices. You should expect each user to require between 2 and 4 megabytes of virtual storage for the system.

The complex relationship between virtual storage and real computer memory is far beyond the scope of this book. Suffice it to say that in IBM operating systems each user may have a maximum of either 16 megabytes or 2 gigabytes of virtual storage (depending on the operating system and the CPU model), regardless of the amount of real storage in the CPU. However, the CPU and disk resources required by users increase with the amount of virtual storage defined for each. Consequently, the management of the computer facility may not be inclined to give each user of an on-line text system the maximum amount of virtual storage. Most shops set limits of 2 to 3 megabytes per user, and you may have to negotiate this value upwards.

On-line Storage

On-line storage is disk or *Direct Access Storage Device* (DASD) storage. We stated above that at least a gigabyte (1 billion bytes) of disk storage would be needed. This is because text takes up quite a lot of room. It can be compressed, but only at the expense of CPU time to compress and decompress it. A billion characters of storage is actually not much these days. The chart in Figure 4-4 shows the capacity of the most common IBM disk devices. Most IBM CPU installations now have at least several of the 3380-DD type of disks, each with its 5.04 GB capacity, and many have installed the triple density 3380-TD models.

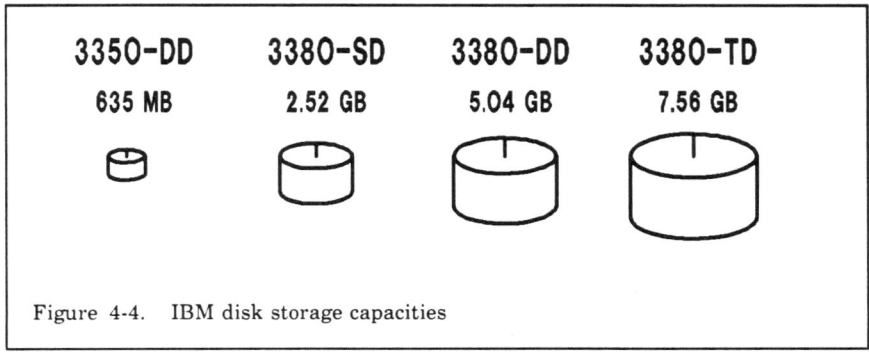

Figure 4-4. IBM disk storage capacities

3380s come in several *models* whose names indicate the type and capacity of individual device. We have simplified that into the SD, DD, and TD designations for *Single Density*, *Double Density*, and *Triple Density*, respectively. These are *not* IBM's actual model designations.

How your text information is stored is the largest factor in determining how much DASD space your system requires. If uncompressed, most documents formatted for on-line viewing require about 1 megabyte for every 400 display screens. Indexes and meta-information related to the text, such as HyperText links or library directories, occupy between 10 and 50% of the amount of space used by the text. This is one reason why it is so important to evaluate the access method and its resource requirements before implementation.

Optical Disk Technology In the last few years we have seen the appearance of optical disk technology, which originated as an audio consumer product in the form of the compact digital disc, is a new form of very high density storage which is particularly applicable to on-line text access systems.

Unfortunately, no products are currently available that connect directly to an IBM mainframe today. There are no optical 3380 DASD. Rather, you must assemble a system wherein the optical disk drives are connected to workstations which are, in turn, attached to a Local Area Network and then *gatewayed* into the mainframe.

As described in *Optical Storage* on page 25, optical disks come in two main types:

- Compact Disc-Read Only Memory (CD-ROM)

- Write Once, Read Many (WORM) disks

CD-ROM is suitable for mass distribution of reference material, but is unchangeable by the user. It uses optical discs which are virtually identical to those used for audio recording; a maximum of about 556 MB per disk is available. CD-ROM is gaining acceptance in markets where large amounts of reference material need to be published and distributed to a broad readership.

WORM storage is suitable for archival and retrieval of text, graphics, and image, but nothing can ever be deleted. Once data is written to a WORM drive, the area of the disk used to hold that data can never be erased or reclaimed. By manipulating the optical disk's directory, such data can be made to disappear, that is, become generally unavailable, but the actual data always resides on the disk. This fact can be used to provide version control over documents which must be replaced periodically.

WORM drives have an idiosyncrasy: while storage and retrieval can occur on both sides of a WORM disk, the drives which do so only access one side at a time. This means that the disk must be physically turned over to access the other half of the data, which requires a *jukebox*.

Systems can be built which treat the text on disks which are currently inserted in drives as *on-line* and the text on disks which are stored in the jukebox racks as *near-line*. The user is only aware of the status of the text as on- or near-line by virtue of the retrieval time. Whenever any text document is accessed on the optical disk, it is moved to a magnetic disk, usually on the optical drive's file server, then sent upstream to the mainframe terminal. The document is moved to the magnetic disk because optical disks, while being an order of magnitude more dense than magnetic disks, are also significantly slower. Migrating a working copy of a document to magnetic disk dramatically improves system performance. If the software searches the magnetic disk first, it is possible for multiple readers to share a single copy of a document and for it to be effectively *on-line* even though its optical disk has been returned to the rack within the jukebox.

Near-line Storage

Near-line storage is the term used to describe storage which is not immediately available, but which can become available to the system automatically and quickly. Your system may not have any of this type of storage since it typically requires specialized hardware and software.

Two examples of near-line storage systems are Automated Tape Libraries (ATL) and Hierarchically Archived Datasets. Automated Tape libraries are devices which can hold several hundred IBM 3480 tape cartridges and are connected to one or more IBM 3480 tape drives. These ATLs use robotics to locate, extract, load, and read data from the tape cartridges. To a user, the data may appear to be on-line because there is no manual intervention required to retrieve it—just a longer time lag before it is presented. This time lag and the fact that the data was not immediately available to the system define this type of storage as *near-line*.

Hierarchically Archived Datasets are disk files that have been copied to specially dedicated DASD in a compressed format. The operating system retrieves these files when their names are referenced, but must decompress them and copy them back to disks which are generally accessible. Again, the user sees no difference in terms of effort, but there is a longer time lag before the text is available.

Another form of near-line storage is discussed later in this chapter when we talk about optical disk storage systems.

58 On-line Text Management

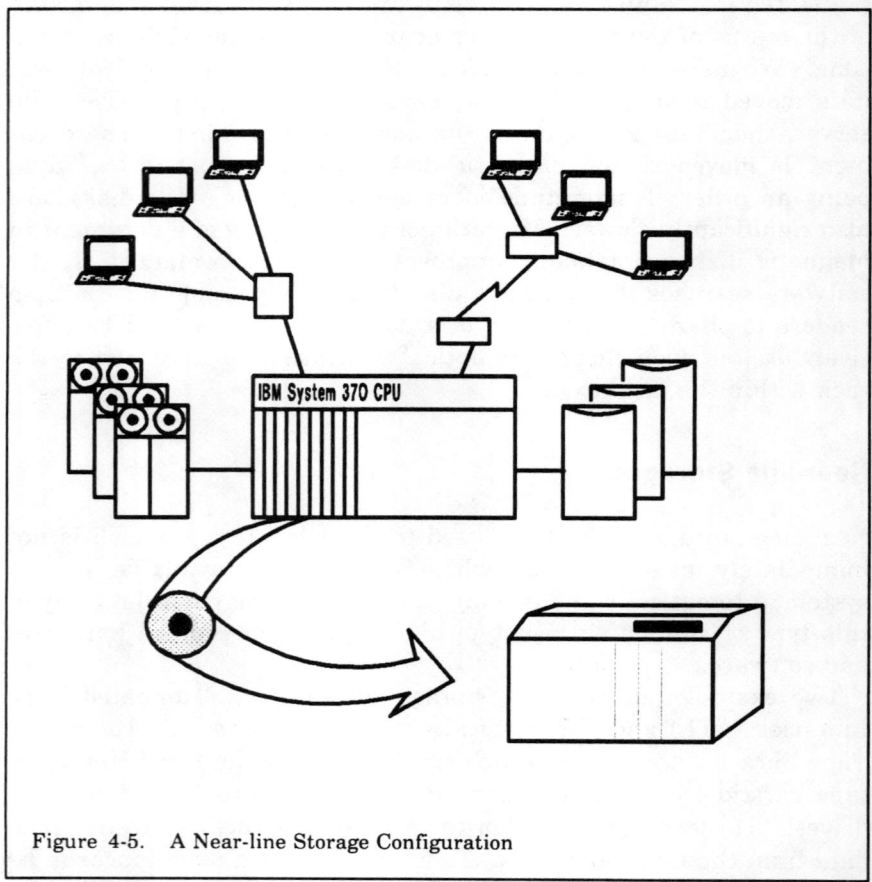

Figure 4-5. A Near-line Storage Configuration

Off-line Storage

Data in off-line storage is not automatically available to the user. It requires human intervention to be loaded and restored. Typically, off-line storage consists of backup or archive tape files which must be restored to the text access system through some external utility program. For example, a restore facility.

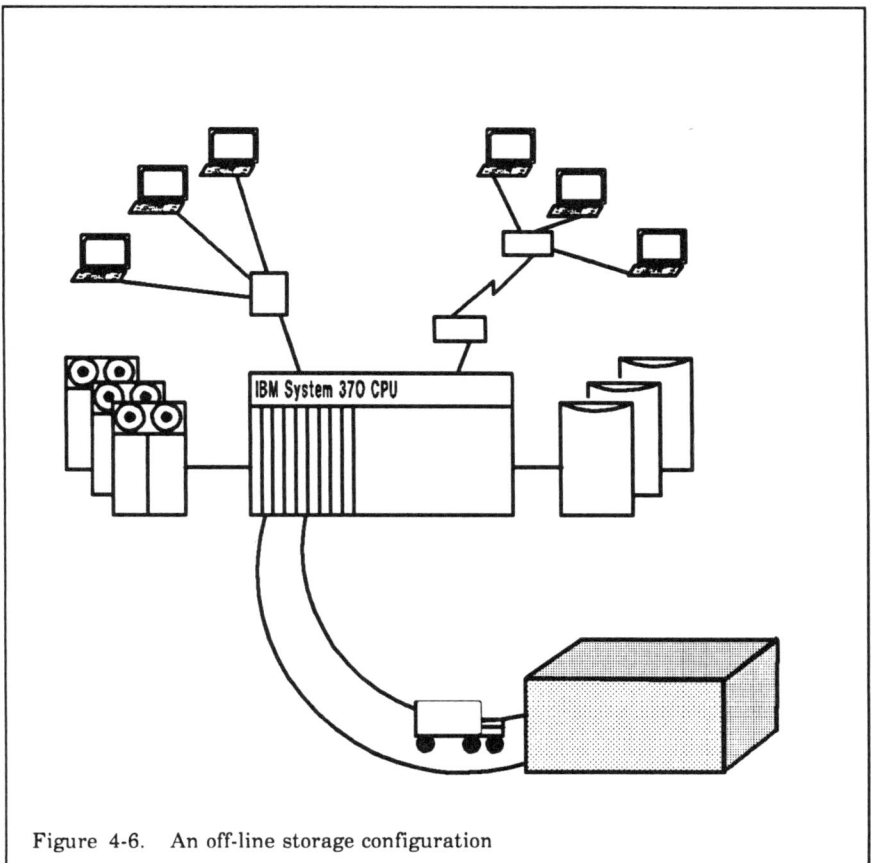

Figure 4-6. An off-line storage configuration

What distinguishes off-line and near-line, from a user's point of view, is the time it takes to retrieve the desired text. Off-line storage can take an hour, a day, or even a week to retrieve, particularly if the backup or archive tapes are stored off-site at a data storage facility. Users should be made aware of the fact that they are about to activate a manual retrieval process so they can, perhaps, reconsider their request. Also, since the retrieval time may be substantial during their training, they should be made aware of the probable time lag for retrieval of off-line text.

Terminals

IBM computing environments typically include a variety of terminal devices of the types listed above and may also include offerings from third-party vendors which are compatible to some degree with those listed. What type of terminals are really required for an effective on-line text access system?

Text-only Terminals

We believe that, in IBM mainframe arenas, on-line text access systems should be designed to operate effectively and efficiently on text-only terminals, such as the *3278*. While there is a growing community of IBM mainframe graphics users, the CPU overhead represented by graphics manipulation is too great for many users to justify. Therefore, any system you design or evaluate should provide sufficient power and functionality with text-only terminals that it can still be used effectively.

At the same time, it should take advantage of color terminals when they are present, as this adds no appreciable CPU overhead, and it should support graphics on graphics-capable devices. An IBM host-based on-line text display system should not require graphics capabilities to be useful, but it should exploit the capabilities of those devices where they are available and when the user requires it.

The system you implement should make use of terminal facilities to indicate different text emphasis. Even for text-only terminals, most IBM devices now offer underlining, reverse video, or blinking.

We advise you to avoid blinking text except where absolutely warranted—that is to say, almost never. Blinking text is distracting and is effective only when a user needs some indication that a long-running process is continuing. In such cases, blinking text provides motion to the screen without any associated CPU overhead.

When using text-only terminals, you need some facility within your text access system to indicate where graphics would appear if a graphics terminal were used or on the paper output. Often a 1- or 2-line description of the graphic suffices when the graphic itself cannot be displayed. Reserving blank space for a graphic which cannot be displayed is typically fruitless and leads to empty or nearly empty screens of text. Try to avoid this by having the text composed for different display devices and selecting the appropriate text file based on terminal device type. Alternatively, if you have little or no need for graphics, dispense with them altogether, leaving only text indicators of their presence. Even if you have graphics terminals, this improves the system response time dramatically and simplifies your programming effort for writing systems in-house.

Color

Use color terminals as often as possible. Given the decline in cost of such devices, you should strongly consider replacing any monochrome terminals you have with color if they are to be used for text access. Color provides the easiest, cheapest, and most readable text differentiation process available on IBM mainframes. Color terminals all have the extended highlighting facilities of underlining and reverse video, which can be combined to offer about 14 different levels of text highlighting.

When choosing colors for your text displays, be cautious and remember the tiring effect bright colors can have on the eye. Try turquoise, white, or green for the majority of text, saving the brighter pinks, reds, and yellows for special emphasis.

You may want to experiment with coloring the background with a solid color like white and presenting the text on it in black, but our experience indicates that this is unacceptable for long-term viewing. The screen colors are too bright to serve as backgrounds, and the IBM terminals tend to warp and bend the screen image when too much reverse video text is displayed.

The designer of a computer system will make choices for colors which seem logical and desirable in the development lab. In the real world of system use, a solid cyan background may not be the best choice. Where possible, *profiles* which allow such things as the colors to be chosen by each individual user should be available. Profiles are usually small disk files of commands which the system reads and executes during initialization. They need to be simple enough that each user can modify them to suit personal tastes.

Graphics and WYSIWYG

While we have stated that graphics and graphics terminals are not necessary for a well-designed and well-implemented on-line text access system, if you need or can afford graphics, put them in your system requirements. Just be aware of the potential CPU, hardware, and software cost.

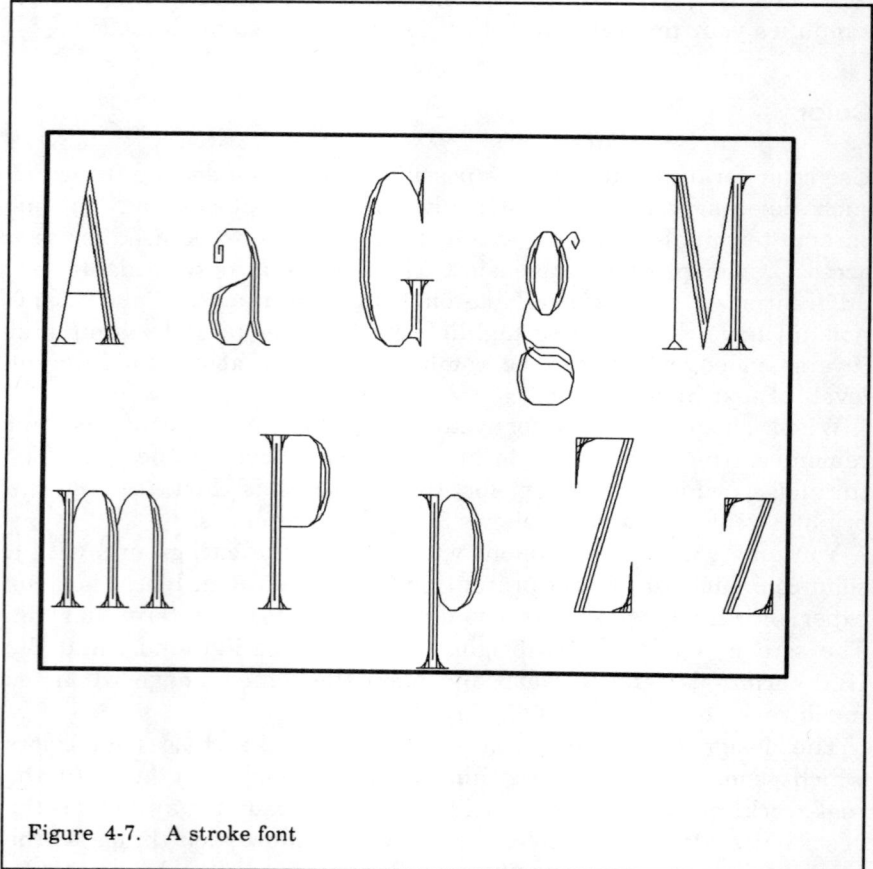

Figure 4-7. A stroke font

You should also be aware that there are two types of computer-generated graphics: *vector* and *raster*. Vector graphics are those which consist of a series of drawing instructions. The instructions may tell a graphics processing program to draw a straight line between two points or to draw an arc through three points. Raster graphics, on the other hand, consist of a rectangular array of on and off dots. These dots require no interpretation since they map directly onto a display screen's surface or onto a laser printed page.

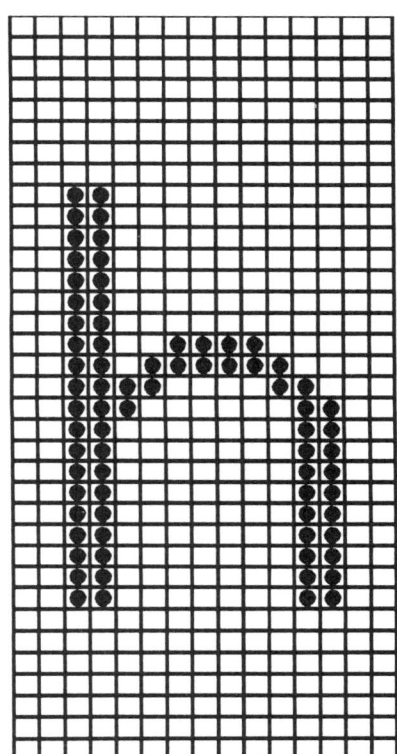

Figure 4-8. A bitmap font

Vector graphics files are usually much smaller than equivalent raster graphics files, but vectors require interpretation. Most graphics packages, such as GDDM, produce both formats, but lean toward vector files.

In this discussion we treat What-You-See-Is-What-You-Get (WYSIWYG) displays of text as a special case of graphics applications. Most IBM terminals must display text as vectors, not rasters, even though the final display is a raster screen image. host-attached IBM host-attached graphics terminals use GDDM to display WYSIWYG images, and GDDM does not handle this function efficiently. This is beginning to change with the introduction of 3193 image terminals, but these cannot handle the more common graphics such as business charts or Computer Aided Design (CAD) drawings.

WYSIWYG text can be displayed on IBM graphics terminals, such as the 3192-G, in two ways:

- By drawing a picture of a page of text using vector-based *stroke fonts*. (See Figure 4-7 on page 62.) This is what the IBM *BrowseMaster* product does. Since each character must be scaled as it is being drawn, this is very time consuming and CPU intensive.

- By displaying a bitmap image of a page of text that was either scanned or imaged in memory. (See Figure 4-8 on page 63.) This process works well with 3193s and can be emulated by 3179-G or 3192-G terminals, but the resolution of those graphics terminals is so low that only a fraction of a page of text can be displayed and still be readable.

The fraction is larger for a PS/2 with the 8514 display, but even that device does not offer sufficient resolution for a full-page display.

The best graphics solution for IBM mainframes is that of the graphics workstation, typically represented by the PS/2 running the Graphics Workstation Program or the (now obsolete) PC/AT-GX running the Graphics Control Program. The latter is no longer sold by IBM, but many IBM systems already have these, and they have a very loyal following among their users.

Graphics on IBM mainframes require quite a lot of computing power, even when much of the work is downloaded into workstations. This is a very good reason to consider a dedicated CPU for your on-line text facility if you cannot afford the impact a heavy graphics and text application might pose on your CPU. You might also consider limiting the use of graphics in your text access system to only a few users or only the occasional picture.

A new technique for managing the graphics overhead in mainframe environments has appeared in the last few years. It may become the solution of choice; move the graphics completely off the mainframe. This is accomplished by having the workstations connected to each other in a Local Area Network (LAN) as well as to the mainframe. Graphics are all stored on the LAN's file servers and are available only to LAN users. They can be intermixed with

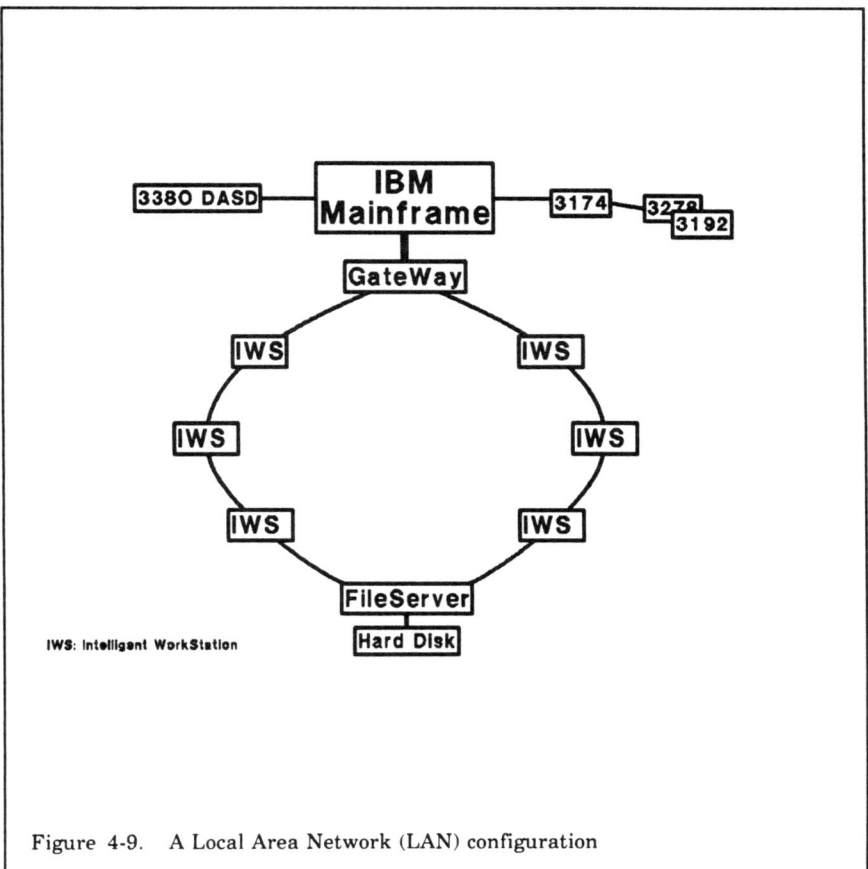

Figure 4-9. A Local Area Network (LAN) configuration

text from the mainframe by specialized software on the PC or PS/2 computers attached to the LAN.

Resolution can be improved on the PS/2 workstations by using third-party vendors' monitors, many of which can display full pages of text in WYSIWYG fonts. Alternatively, you can use other vendor's workstations with connectivity software which allows them to emulate 3270 terminals attached to either the mainframe or a LAN.

These are very sophisticated and expensive systems, however, and any further discussion of them would digress, to some degree, from the topic of this book. It is an option to be considered, however, particularly in light of the connectivity issue discussed in the next section on Optical Disks.

To wrap up our discussion of terminal requirements for on-line text systems, let us say once again that we feel it is possible to build a viable, usable, efficient, and powerful text access system on mainframe computers without resorting to terminals that provide graphics or WYSIWYG font support. For most applications, text access systems need only be concerned with text.

We do advocate the use of color, particularly for indicating emphasis in text. We caution against the overuse of either color or extended highlighting, however. Blinking text should particularly be avoided except in the cases mentioned above.

Graphics and WYSIWYG text are fine and very desirable, but they are expensive in the IBM mainframe arena. If you absolutely need them, then you must afford both the terminals and the CPU overhead associated with them. If you can afford the terminals and the CPU power, we advise making graphics and WYSIWYG available, as they enhance the functionality of a text access system considerably. But do not rule out implementation of an on-line text facility simply because the powerful graphics abilities seen on other vendors' workstations are not available. Much of that is flash and unnecessary to the purpose at hand: that of presenting textual information in a usable and efficient manner.

System Requirements Review

A powerful on-line text access system can be built around existing mainframe technology. There are limitations, particularly with respect to graphics and WYSIWYG text display, but mainframe systems are very well suited since so most of the required facilities already exists in most shops:

- A powerful CPU

- Appropriate interactive computing system software

- A network of interactive display terminals

- A large amount of disk storage

This is especially true in terms of presenting textual information to the user. More sophisticated systems are possible with the addition of:

- Advanced, color terminals
- Graphics power in both terminals and CPU
- Local Area Networks
- Optical disk storage
- File servers

If you are seriously considering the implementation of an on-line text system, carefully study the existing environment. Ensure that the minimum requirements we have outlined, and any other requirements your application may have, are met. With these conditions met, you should conclude that most of the desired features can be implemented without massive changes and expenditures.

Part

2

Directions in Text Access

In this section we review more of the considerations behind introducing an on-line text management system to a user population. We also look at the more traditional uses of text stored on mainframes, from informational messages for the terminal user to programmed instruction. This discussion provides a baseline for the more intriguing uses of text stored in a mainframe environment.

Chapter

5

Text Access Methods Yesterday and Today

When you look about your existing mainframe environment, you should find that your users are already presented with on-line information from your system and application programs in a variety of ways:

- Application and System Program Error Messages
- Specific Text Mapping
- Context-Sensitive Text Mapping
- On-line Tutorials
- Computer-based Instruction

To better understand what a good on-line text access and management system can add to your business environment, you should understand how far you have already come. As we begin this overview, remember that early methods of providing information back to the user, either interactively or in an error report, required mapping of an event in the program to explanatory text. As we look at the evolution of text access, we again use this concept of mapping to explain how events, such as requesting more information about an error, are linked to the text.

Error Messages

Many application and system programmers did not put steps into their programs to interpret error conditions; they allowed the program to terminate with an *ABnormal END* (ABEND) and stop processing without any information about what caused the problem. The only way to find the problem was to pour through mounds of paper in hope that you could find where the bad information entered the system. You then hoped that you could change it.

From ABENDs as the only method of passing information about problem data passed to a program, the next evolutionary step was to add code to validate the data coming into the program environment. If the information did not fit a given criteria, a message was generated and routed either to a print file for batch programs or to the terminal screen for interactive programs. In many programs the error message was limited to a reference number that could be looked up in a manual. More in-depth applications generated a message number and some text, although the usefulness of the text depended on the writing skills of the programmer. It was not uncommon to find messages that said little more than *Error Condition*. No more meaningful, but more helpful, were messages which generated a reference to a specific manual or that generated some type of code which could be used to identify a specific problem.

The next obvious step was to provide meaningful text within the message, even if it must span more than one line. There are still many programs which generate multi-line informational messages. These lengthier messages are generally more helpful because they can indicate the source of the problem, and often suggest a solution.

We have used the past tense throughout most of this explanation, but in fact this is the point at which many host-based application systems are today. This is especially true of systems designed many years ago that have been modified but never re-written. At this point in the evolution of on-line information, the user must still move into an off-line environment to get any additional help with the error condition.

While it takes more programming, and a bit more thought and effort on the part of the designers and programmers, the next step is to add truly meaningful messages to the program environment. In fact, a two-tiered approach is commonly found in interactive systems:

```
TUTORIAL --------------- GENERAL INFORMATION -------- INVALID SELECTION
OPTION   ===> FORWARD
                              --------------------------
                              |    GENERAL INFORMATION    |
                              --------------------------

ISPF operates on the IBM 3270 and 3290 display terminals.  It
uses panels to allow you to select options and to specify parameters,
commands and program function (PF) keys to simplify requests for
common functions, and full-screen format for information display and
editing.  When data does not fit on the screen, ISPF provides
scrolling in all four directions.

ISPF supports the display of graphic images on ISPF panels by
allowing dialogs to interface with the Graphical Data Display
Manager (GDDM) Program Product.  ISPF also contains the mechanisms
that permit a dialog, during its execution, to determine or change
the format and contents of an ISPF panel.

The following topics are presented in sequence, or may be selected
by number:
    1 - Display formats           6 - Output listings
    2 - Commands and PF keys      7 - 3270/3290 display terminals
    3 - PA keys                   8 - Dynamic formatting
    4 - Scrolling                 9 - ISPF/GDDM interface
    5 - Split screen mode
```

Figure 5-1. On screen message indicating invalid selection: The message, in the top right corner of the screen, warns that an invalid selection was made from the ISPF tutorial panel, which is included with the IBM ISPF program product.

- Tier 1: The initial message which indicates that an error has occurred.

- Tier 2: An additional message, which the user must request, which provides a bit more information.

When this technique is used, it is possible for an experienced user to immediately understand the problem and take the appropriate actions to correct it. A less experienced user can request more help using a command or function key. The messages are usually displayed in a message area at the top or bottom of the screen.

It is from this background that the path from an error message to a full-screen on-line help facility evolves. On-line help, which we

```
TUTORIAL ------------------ GENERAL INFORMATION ----------- INVALID SELECTION
OPTION  ===> FORWARD
VALID CODES ARE B, S, U, T OR I, OR A NUMBER IF SELECTION LIST PRESENT.
                        |  GENERAL INFORMATION  |
                        -------------------------

    ISPF operates on the IBM 3270 and 3290 display terminals.  It
    uses panels to allow you to select options and to specify parameters,
    commands and program function (PF) keys to simplify requests for
    common functions, and full-screen format for information display and
    editing.  When data does not fit on the screen, ISPF provides
    scrolling in all four directions.

    ISPF supports the display of graphic images on ISPF panels by
    allowing dialogs to interface with the Graphical Data Display
    Manager (GDDM) Program Product.  ISPF also contains the mechanisms
    that permit a dialog, during its execution, to determine or change
    the format and contents of an ISPF panel.

    The following topics are presented in sequence, or may be selected
    by number:
        1 - Display formats            6 - Output listings
        2 - Commands and PF keys       7 - 3270/3290 display terminals
        3 - PA keys                    8 - Dynamic formatting
        4 - Scrolling                  9 - ISPF/GDDM interface
        5 - Split screen mode
```

Figure 5-2. Screen message expanded to informational message on third line: The additional message shown on the third line of the panel displays when the user requests more information with the PF1 function key.

consider to be a form of *specific text mapping*, is the first step in providing true on-line text access, albeit in primitive form.

Specific Text Mapping

By *specific text mapping* we mean the mapping of text to an application in such a way that the user can access it from within the application. Typically only one text file (document) is accessed, and access begins at the top of the file. The text may concern only a portion of the application or may describe the entire application. It is not necessarily context-sensitive.

On-line help is the most common form of specific text mapping. For example, from most IBM host-based systems you can use the **PF1** key to display help screens. The information that displays depends on the application that is active at the time: operating system, text editor, or user application. A menu may display to further narrow the type of help you require, or the programming may be designed so that you receive very high-level help about an overall function with no direct path to further help.

For example, if you press **PF1** from within an XEDIT session under CMS, a menu of topics concerning XEDIT displays. You may select one of these topics to see its associated help text. As shown in Figure 5-3 on page 76, within the help text file you may scroll forward and backward as needed; when you are through with the help text, **PF3** returns you to the menu. You must use **PF3** again to return to where the help was originally called. There is no direct path from one help file to another, even when they are related topics.

Ultimately you access text based on a menu topic or based on where you are in the overall environment. You cannot request that only the information related to the task you need to perform be displayed: you must perform the search through all of the information presented. The amount of information available, and its organization, is limited to what the help system developer put into the single file and, perhaps, references to other files or off-line information (paper copies of manuals).

When references are made to other files, the user is responsible for exiting the current screen and accessing the referenced file. No automatic links to those files are provided.

Another type of specific text mapping provides access to an entire manual in an on-line environment. The access is considered specific since the path into the document is from within an application. The application may be as simple as a front end to provide easy user access to the document, or a functional application such as a materials requirements planning or order entry system that includes an exit to the on-line manual instead of, or in addition to, a help system.

For example, from an accounts receivable system you might have access to the user guide by entering a command or pressing a function key. In another case a company policy document may be available on-line which details the company policies regarding vacations, sick leave, and the various forms required to request office supplies, make travel arrangements, and to fill out expense reports.

```
    --> GSI DCF <-----> HELP   INFORMATION <------>line ---> 1 of 223
    The DCF EXEC

    Use the DCF EXEC to execute IBM's Document Composition
    Facility (DCF) and handle the output from it in a
    variety of ways.  DCF EXEC  can:

       - invoke a post-processor such as our DCF/PLUS
       - retain your options information, including fonts
       - retain your DCF output in a disk file
       - retain your output to your reader

    DCF EXEC is a full-screen CMS/DMS application and can save
    your screen variables in any user defined variable groups.
    When DCF is started, you have the opportunity to specify
    which GROUP (or environment) you wish to have the screen
    restored from.

    The format of the DCF EXEC is:

    ----------------------------------------------------------------
    |          |  |                                             |
    |DCF       |  | <font1 font2 ...> < ( <oldgroup> <newgroup> > |
    |          |  | -                                           -
    ----------------------------------------------------------------
      1- All       2- Top      3- Quit   4- Return     5- Clocate        6- ?
      7- Backward  8- Forward  9- PFkey  10- Backward 1/2  11- Forward 1/2  12- Cursor

    ---->
                                                    Macro-read 1 File
```

Figure 5-3. Function-specific help from the CMS Help System

While this on-line access is nice, locating specific information can become time consuming. If there is an accurate table of contents or index, the task is easier, but if there are multiple references, you must note each and move to each independently.

While specific text mapping provides more access to more information than simple help screens, the user of the on-line document is still responsible for developing and executing a search plan. There is no defined plan of attack, and it is up to the user to note each file reviewed in case there is a need to return to the previously viewed information for clarification.

Context-sensitive Text Access

The term *context-sensitive* arrives in the second wave of serious attempts to provide on-line help and text access. The goal of a context-sensitive text access system is to be aware of the context in which the help was requested and to provide a direct path to all relevant entries in the text file.

While providing the raw text of a user manual was not difficult, system designers (particularly those of microcomputer products) rapidly became aware that when someone used a help key, something less than the entire manual but more than a single error message was desired.

This process is not trivial. Determining which piece of help text the user requires is often an exercise in disambiguation and can be complicated if the designer tries to provide more intelligence in the help system than necessary. For instance, when a user asks for help from a particular screen, it is fairly simple to access a screen of text linked to the screen currently in use by the system. But if the designers want to offer more intelligence, help text might be accessed based on the *field* the cursor is in. If the user actually wants information about a different, but related, field, or if the cursor is between fields, it may not be possible to provide context-sensitive help.

Systems based on the use of context-sensitive help text are very popular—so much so that they have led to the development of context-sensitive text access systems which are not based on help text, but on reference text. There are on-line reference manuals which organize the presentation of materials based on the context within which it was requested. Determining the context and the associated text can still pose problems, but these systems get better with each new product. The best designed systems include a table of contents, index, or other topic location scheme to provide a method for developing a search pattern.

We discuss the technical considerations of developing this type of system in a later chapter.

On-line Tutorials

The next step, or really a concurrent step, is to provide some on-line education about an application. This type of application is typically closer in nature to an on-line user's guide than to help text. Tuto-

78 On-line Text Management

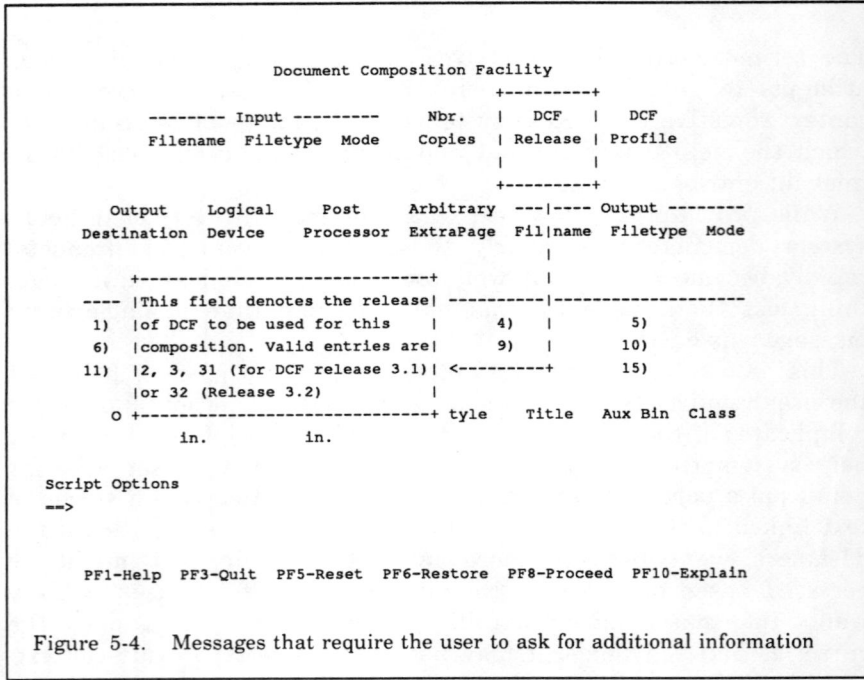

Figure 5-4. Messages that require the user to ask for additional information

rials are accessed by a command sequence or through a menu system. Access to the tutorial may be independent of the application or from within it.

Tutorials are constructed so that the user is guided from topic to topic in a directed manner, building on the knowledge presented. Each lesson may be a single file which is accessed independently, or may cause the next file (lesson) to be accessed automatically. There is rarely any type of bookmark capability, which places the burden of remembering start and stop points on the user.

Overall, on-line tutorials on the mainframe are nothing more than on-line users guides that incorporate some type of baseline feature, such as exercises or tests. These tests are not always interactive, though. The answers are often located in another file that must be viewed independently, or reside in an off-line manual. The primary function of an on-line tutorial is to provide education about an on-line application in the same medium as the application.

Computer-based Instruction

The next step in on-line text access and education is *computer-based instruction* (CBI), which implies an interactive nature to the system. There are volumes devoted to the design and implementation of computer-based instruction systems, and it is not our mission in this book to provide specific instructions or discuss specific considerations surrounding this type of text access. We do mention it, though, because many of the design and implementation considerations which surround computer-based instruction are applicable to on-line text access. If you have designed and implemented computer-based instruction, or even investigated the feasibility of adding such a capability to your environment, many of the management decisions will seem familiar.

In general, computer based instruction involves access to an interactive education environment. The user is normally required to read a passage of on-line text and then work through exercises. The answers to the exercises are typically interpreted immediately, providing quick feedback. Most systems are linear in nature, which means that it is not possible to look at an index of topics covered and access only those passages and exercises which apply to a specific problem.

The Next Step

The history of on-line access, from simple error messages to more sophisticated on-line text access, lays the groundwork for the areas we intend to cover in depth: new text access methods incorporating hypertext concepts and more. You will discover, as we did, that once you reach context-sensitive text access, the technology to make that access more flexible is not far away.

Chapter

6

New Approaches to Accessing Text

In this section we discuss several of the new approaches to text access that have appeared in the last few years. The topics we cover are:

- Associative text navigation
- HyperText
- HyperMedia

We start with an overview of the new methods of displaying text on the terminal that have become popular with the advent of a variety of popular software packages for PC-based products and that are now freely emulated by mainframe-based products.

New Presentation Methods

New methods of displaying and working with text in computerized environments began to appear during the last 10 years. Most began in the PC arena, but mainframe users exposed to both environments began to demand more user-friendly interfaces for their products, too. These interfaces include:

- **Windowing**.
  A window is an area on the terminal that permits the display of related information while the core application is still viewable on the screen. This allows the user to retain the context in which the secondary information was requested, as shown in Figure 6-1.

```
                         HyperText Research Project
+------------------------------------------------+      +---------------+
| HyperDoc: IPLPROC                              |      |     Help      |
|                                                |      | PF1 - Help    |
|                                                |      | PF2 - Links   |
| GSI IPL Procedure - 04/01/88                   |      | PF3 - Quit    |
|                                                |      | PF4 - Bk 1/2  |
| Operating Systems and Their Names              |      | PF5 - Fd 1/2  |
| There are four operating systems which must    |      | PF6 - Locate  |
| be IPL'd in order to bring GSI's computing     |      | PF7 - Back    |
| facilities fully online. In addition, the CPU  |      | PF8 - Frwd    |
| itself must be dealt with on occasion. For     |      | PF10- First   |
| simplicity, this document will refer to  each  |      | PF11- Last    |
| of  these  systems by a unique acronym. These  |      | PF12- Level1  |
| Level: 1                      Line: 1 of 656   |      | ENT - Close   |
+------------------------------------------------+      +---------------+
```

Figure 6-1. Window interface example: This screen illustrates two functional windows on a standard 3270-type terminal.

Many windowing strategies have developed, but one of the most popular is the *desktop paradigm*, where windows appear as overlapping sheets of paper on a desktop.

```
                   Expert System Research Project
   File     Go      Stop     Edit    Help     Trace     Configure     Reply
  +------------------------------------------+---------+------------+
  | STOP                                     | Windows |            |
  | COMPILE SOME11.KB.B1                +--------+ Speed   |            |
  | SHOW KB                             | Save   | Verbose |            |
  | SHOW KB                             | Load   | Listing |            |
  | ERROR: "02" is an invalid attribute value | Alter  | Close   |            |
  |         (Valid values are   4 - 11.) +------------------------+            |
  | STOP                                     | Create Window          |            |
  |                                          | Delete Window          |            |
  | RUN                                      | Select Stream Colors   |            |
  | Your answer was : Blue  , with a cer | Select Window Contents |            |
  | %CONFIGURE TEMPLATES BRIEF               | Change Screen Title    |            |
  |                                          | Change Color Selection |            |
  |                                          | Close                  |            |
  |                                          | Quit                   |            |
  +------------------------------------------+------------------------+---------+
  | What is your favorite color?             | Blue                            |
  |                                          | Yellow                          |
  |                                          | I don't know that...            |
  |                                          |Previous                         |
  |                                          |Next                             |
  |                                          |                                 |
  |                                          |                                 |
  +------------------------------------------+---------------------------------+
  Command: %CONFIGURE ........................................................
```

Figure 6-2. Pull-down menu example: This screen illustrates a window with a menu bar at the top. The user selects a function by tabbing to it on the menu bar and pressing the ENTER key. In this example the CONFIGURE example was selected, then the WINDOW function was selected from the CONFIGURE menu.

- **Pull-down or pop-up menus.**
  The concept of a menu of potential choices that can easily appear and disappear has drastically changed the way in which many people deal with computers. Pull-down menus are typically activated by placing the cursor on a field in a bar along the

top or side of the screen and using the **ENTER** key, or a function key to select the menu. The menu normally overlays the screen image area with its list of functions, as shown in Figure 6-2.

A pop-up menu works in the same fashion. These menus are always available at the touch of a button or key, but occupy screen real estate only when necessary.

Each of these presentation methods is readily available in personal computing environments. They are now appearing in mainframe applications as well. Their impact on on-line text display will be dramatic and positive.

Associative Navigation

Text-based research, especially through reference materials, is generally an associative process. When you have only a small amount of information about a topic, you begin perusing your reference materials by looking for those topics you have already associated to your domain. If you know you want to work on your car, you begin with an auto manual. From there, if you know that the steering needs work, you proceed to the steering section of the manual, generally by using the table of contents. If the information there is insufficient, you may proceed to the index to look for other references to *steering*.

A word or phrase in the steering section, however, may prompt you to look elsewhere. If the steering section mentions that misalignment of the wheels can cause steering problems, you may scan for *alignment* in the index and turn to that section of the manual. This is associative navigation.

Associative navigation text access systems have several important characteristics that distinguish them from the methods introduced previously. Some of these characteristics also limit the applicability of such systems and point the way to further advances in text access technology. These distinguishing characteristics are:

- **The text is static.**
  The text is unchanging and organized in a linear fashion. Regardless of the order of associations that locate a particular passage, the sequence of the text is always going to be the same around a given keyword.

- **Graphics are static.**
  Associative searches for a graphic are actually conducted against the text that is associated with the graphic: captions, for instance.

- **Keyword searches are conducted by the user.**
  Users are responsible for maintaining all associations in their own minds or having those associations triggered by reading the text. The associative indexing process has no inherent intelligence that allows it to *know* whether an association is significant or not.

- **Access is freer.**
  This happens because each non-noise word can be a keyword for search purposes. A *noise word* is a word which must normally be indexed but does not lend anything to the search process, such as a preposition or an article.

- **Associative access systems do not provide for one document to reference another.**
  All associations are internal to a single document.

- **There is greater freedom to the user to wander around inside a document.**
  Older techniques sometimes limited the users by allowing access to a particular section of text only when a specific type of related error occurred.

- **Associative navigation systems are suitable for more than just help systems.**
  Begining with associative navigation systems, advanced text processing systems can support *demand* text perusal. This makes the implementation of on-line reference and research materials truly possible.

- **Associative navigation allows you to move to different sections of a document at random.**
  The direction and path followed to reach a given reference are no longer static.

- **Documents navigated through associative means still retain their linear nature.**
  The document is still written, or can at least be viewed, so that it makes sense when read from start to finish.
- **Presentation methods for the retrieved text may be very primitive or very sophisticated.**
  This may involve nothing more complex than displaying text on a screen, but can become as sophisticated as merging graphics with proportional text in multiple fonts within different windows.

It is possible to use this technique for scanning and researching on-line text. Through the use of *content-based* or *associative* access methods, on-line text systems have become capable of supporting this type of search at varying levels of detail.

Some systems are keyword-sensitive in the manner that book indexes are. If the particular word or phrase that sparks your associative memory has not been anticipated by the designer, your association is not usable as a search key. Other systems index every significant word and phrase in a document, allowing any association to be used. This technique is sometimes known as *document signature indexing* and requires a search of the full text. These systems tend to produce a lot of *noise* references; information is returned which has nothing to do with the association you are making. This is distracting during a search, although in some systems it is possible to filter out some of the noise by carefully defining the context of the search by adding limiting criteria.

Associative navigation of a text database can be very helpful, but systems that use it exclusively often require the user to spend several weeks gaining familiarity with appropriate search strategies. These strategies depend on how the system was implemented and differ from system to system.

Associative navigation continues to be a popular method in developing text systems because it is a powerful search technique. Refinements have already appeared that use artificial intelligence to provide context and common sense reasoning to the access process.

HyperText Systems

One step beyond simple associative access is HyperText. HyperText systems are commercially available in a variety of environments, although there is still quite a lot of confusion and disagreement over just what HyperText really is. For the purposes of this book, we have defined HyperText in the following manner:

> *HyperText is the concept of accessing and perusing text in a non-linear manner through the use of software links between document elements, as well as through sequential and associative methods.*

As with most technical definitions, this one uses terms that need definition themselves.

First let us look at the term *non-linear*. When you use a reference book, you may encounter forward and backward references to related material. alternatively, you may encounter citations of other works on related topics. Since you are probably after specific information, you page back and forth through the current text, holding your place with a finger or a bookmark. You might even abandon the book you are currently using while you look up a citation in another document. In short, you use the text in a completely non-linear fashion. Indeed, where reference materials are well organized and quickly accessible, this is the most efficient process for locating and exhausting the available information on a topic.

The term *software links* in our HyperText definition describes the pointers between specific locations within a text file and other specific locations within the same or other text files. The concept of links is illustrated in Figure 6-3 on page 88. They are the software instantiation of footnote or bibliographic citations; they simulate the physical process of turning to the referenced page or pulling the cited work from the shelves.

88 On-line Text Management

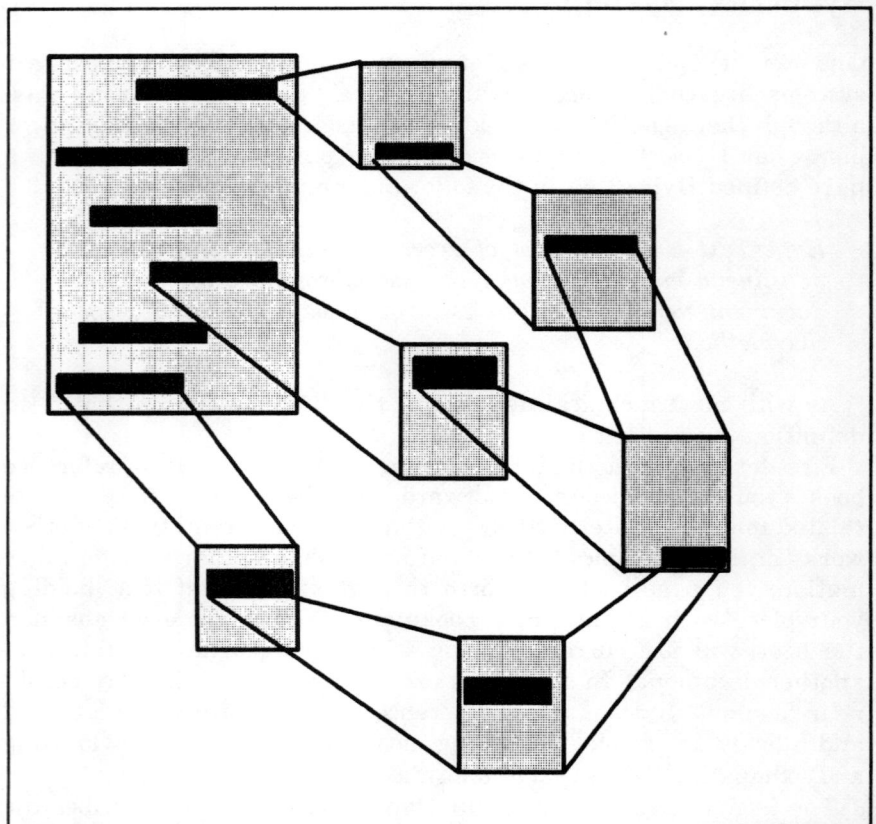

Figure 6-3. Text flow through documents in a HyperText system: Each black box represents a node, which contains links to other text chunks. These chunks may also contain links to other text chunks.

Links are a process as much as they are information. They have names so that multiple links can be attached to a single document element. These can be referenced by a *link type*, which allows referential searches to be narrowed to avoid unnecessary noise in the information retrieved.

Document elements are words, phrases, sentences, paragraphs or other document objects. HyperText systems allow links between such elements to be both internal and external to the document under review.

HyperText links which are internal can also be said to be *intradocument* links; they exist between two places in the *same* document. Conversely, external or *interdocument* links exist between two *different* documents.

Many commercial HyperText systems offer optional features, such as the ability to annotate, place bookmarks, or define new links and link types. As useful as these features are, they can be absent from a system that truly embodies the HyperText concept.

HyperText systems have a variety of distinguishing characteristics:

- **HyperText systems bring the concept of *object-oriented documenting* to the user.**

  Object-oriented documenting is the use of document elements as keys and references to other parts of a document or other documents entirely.

- **HyperText systems do not use only words as keys; the author builds many associations by defining many links.**

  Links with defined link types serve as keys to specific information, providing the author with a way to guide the user to information that is deemed important and related.

- **A single HyperText node such as a word or a phrase may have multiple links emanating from it.**

  These are typically made visible to the user on request so that the appropriate path can be followed.

- **HyperText presentation techniques presume the availability of a windowing environment.**

  HyperText does not work as well if the current node must be overwritten to display the target node. The loss of context is often too devastating. One of the prime concerns of HyperText developers is the management of *screen real estate*. The placement of the next window when a link is selected is critical to the usability of the system.

- **Fully implemented HyperText systems provide much more freedom.**

  They are freer than associative navigation systems because they free the user from the distraction of the *noise* references that go hand-in-hand with systems which use only associative navigation.

- **HyperText systems typically use static text and graphics.**
  Graphics may be very sophisticated if the terminal environment includes high resolution screens, and the text is written to conform to the concept of hypertext browsing. While it can be read sequentially, the movement within the document generated by activating defined links will always take the reader to a section which "makes sense" in the context of the section just read.

- **HyperText systems significantly depart from associative navigation systems in that links can exist between multiple documents.**
  Activating a link may cause an entirely different document to be opened, positioned, and displayed.

- **Documents written specifically to take advantage of the HyperText environment are known as *HyperDocuments*.**
  These are non-linear in organization and often depend heavily on the capability to define links. HyperText systems can be made to work with more traditional documents that are linear in nature. These documents will benefit greatly from being accessible to a HyperText user. The full power of HyperText is not realized, however, until HyperDocuments are included in its structure.

- **HyperDocuments are built from *links* and *nodes*.**
  Links are the programmatic pointers from a place in one document to a place in the same document or in another document. Nodes are the document elements referenced by the links. A word may be linked to another word or phrase, and the link may be two-way. While a given word or phrase in one document may have links pointing to some other place, typically, the target is a higher-level document element, such as a paragraph, a chapter, or a section.

- **HyperText can support HyperDocuments in a two-tier manner.**

  ○ The first tier of HyperText support provides links written by the document author. Without this fundamental property, the system is not HyperText.

○ The second tier of support is the availability of associative searches. This provides users with the freedom of an associative navigation system while still providing the more structured link environment as defined by the document author.

○ The third tier of HyperText support is reached when the system provides the ability for the user to define the links. At this point the system enters a new level of sophistication, because reader-defined links are, in essence, additions to the text; the user is creating the HyperDocument. This provides a vastly greater degree of freedom, particularly when the HyperDocument is shared between users. Now the whole meaning of the document as perceived by second and subsequent users can change from user to user.

- **HyperText, in its management of the HyperDocument, requires that methods of text presentation be redefined.**

    For instance, the manner in which the links are made available to the user, (function keys, menu items) should change depending on the situation in which the user is requesting the information.

HyperMedia

HyperMedia systems are one step beyond HyperText. They embody HyperText as a subset, but require a leap forward in technology to implement. They provide a new way of acquiring knowledge.

HyperMedia systems are distinguished from HyperText systems by the following characteristics:

- **HyperMedia goes beyond management of reading materials.**

    HyperDocuments become much more than just *documents*. HyperMedia systems can manipulate many other presentation media than just text and graphics. They can include links to video displays, animation, and audio recordings, which greatly expands the type of information presented.

- **The text is still static.**

    That is, documents constructed for use within the HyperMedia system remain unchanged by the environment.

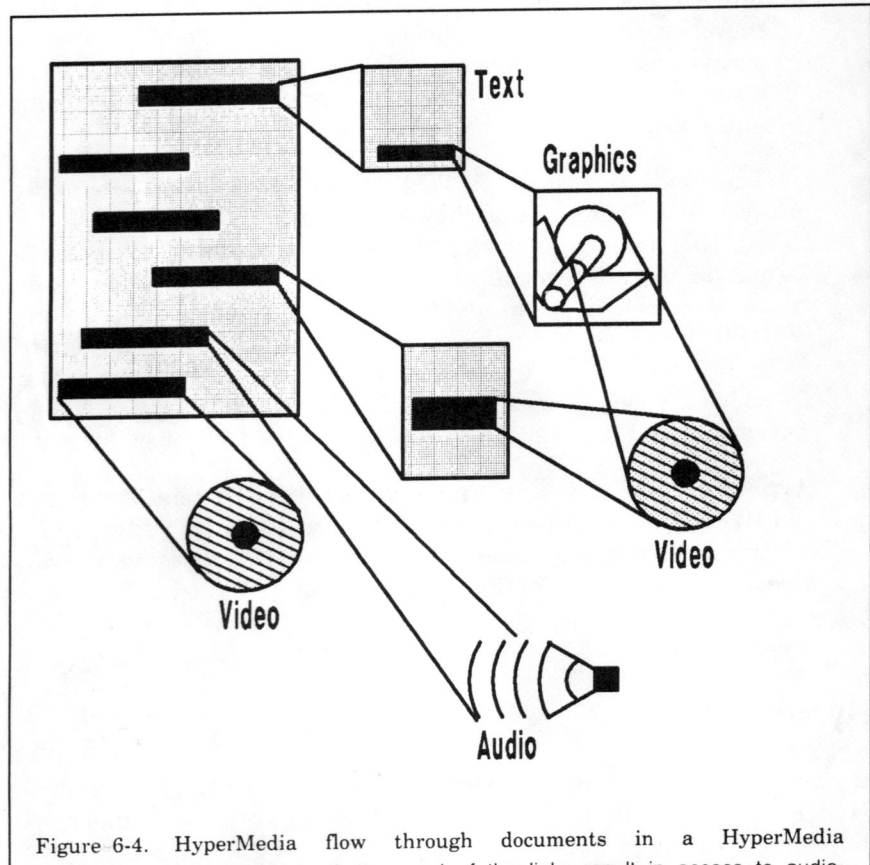

Figure 6-4. HyperMedia flow through documents in a HyperMedia system: Note that several of the links result in access to audio, video, or other non-traditional types of documents.

- **Graphics may be static, but might be animated.**
  Objects displayed in windows may rotate continuously while other areas of the document are researched. Or, the assembly of a product may be shown in animation in one window as the user reviews the text in an adjacent window.

- **Video and audio presentations may accompany the text and computer graphics of HyperMedia systems.**
  It is, in fact, this feature which demands a new name. Video and audio will typically reside on optical disk, often a compact

disc or CD-ROM, connected to the workstation. References to video or audio objects will be through the standard HyperText link process and typically the user is unaware of what type of media a link may invoke. An overview of this process is illustrated in Figure 6-4 on page 92.

A window is opened and a video presentation begins. The video may be static or animated, and presentation quality is equivalent to broadcast television or videotape. Audio may accompany the video or be accessed separately through a link of its own.

- **HyperMedia systems demand multi-tasking workstations**

  Each window that opens must be a separate task with computer processing ongoing while the user examines other windows. If a HyperMedia system is to be implemented in a mainframe environment, it must run on workstations that are connected to the mainframe, probably through a local area network (LAN). Current IBM mainframe technology is insufficient to implement HyperMedia in any economical manner.

- **HyperMedia systems require ultra-high resolution terminals.**

  It should be possible to comfortably view a video presentation or a high resolution engineering drawing in full color in a window no more than 10% the size of the full screen. This is about 18 square inches on a 19-inch monitor. Therefore, a window approximately 4.25 inches on each side should have sufficient resolution for the user to view very fine details in computer generated graphics. A resolution on the order of 200 dots per inch (DPI) should be a requirement of a fully functional HyperMedia system.

- **Since HyperMedia requires the ability to combine video, audio, and data simultaneously, special hardware will be required to manage the screen real estate.**

  Huge amounts of Random Access Memory (RAM) may be required to store a video or audio presentation so that it can be presented while another one is being accessed.

- **HyperMedia systems will almost certainly be built around optical disk storage for text documents**
  The reason for this is economics. Only optical disk offers sufficiently high storage/dollar ratios to make it possible to implement HyperMedia in any usable configuration.

HyperMedia is still a way off as we have described it here. There are systems which begin to implement these concepts, but most of them are still in the research laboratories. Over the next few years, however, you can expect to see HyperMedia systems emerge as the main direction of on-line text in many industries; the medical and engineering industries in particular have great need for such systems.

Selecting the Access Method

Deciding on which of these new access methodologies to use is one of the most important steps in the development of an on-line text system. Coupling them with a very usable human interface is the other. We address the issue of designing the interface in detail in *Evaluation Checklist* on page 107.

It is important to decide early on what the human interface should look like and how it will augment the capabilities of the chosen text access method. For instance, windowing is required for HyperText or HyperMedia, but not for associative navigation systems. How pallettes will appear and operate can significantly affect the usability of a system. You must consider all of these factors as you try to decide what type of text access system to implement.

Chapter 7

What Do You Want from Your Text Access System?

Before you can make intelligent decisions about the type of text access system you would like to add to your business environment, you must evaluate a variety of factors. We looked at some of these factors in earlier chapters. However, in this chapter we want to look at how to do an in-depth evaluation of the type of on-line text access and management system you want and what type you can realistically expect to add to your environment.

Remember at the outset that there are two high-level goals to providing on-line text access:

- Making more information available in a more timely manner to your users.

- Reducing the many costs associated with paper documentation in the business environment.

Almost any application you can think of fits into one of these high goals. For example, the ability to annotate a text, either as part of a review cycle or for personal use, is encompassed by the broadest definition of "making more information available in a more timely manner."

Making More Information More Available

If one of your requirements is to provide a large number of people with various types of information, an on-line system can provide a way to streamline this task. It can also make more information more accessible to a larger population. Information access should not seem like an unusual concern; it does relate directly to employee productivity.

If your employees are working with out-of-date information simply because they have not had the time or inclination to add updated pages to their manuals, you could be losing a fair number of employee hours to recouping the losses from the dissemination of incorrect information.

It does not take much to cause a problem. The problems are multiplied each time a new employee is hired and does not have a complete set of manuals relating to their job, or when someone is missed when manuals are updated.

A change in a company policy toward travel, the change in a replacement part number, or the announcement of a new department head are all pieces of the information puzzle that should be disseminated as quickly as possible to avoid problems. While the traditional method of disseminating information is to get text on paper, make as many copies as required, and then distribute, this is a time-consuming and labor-intensive process.

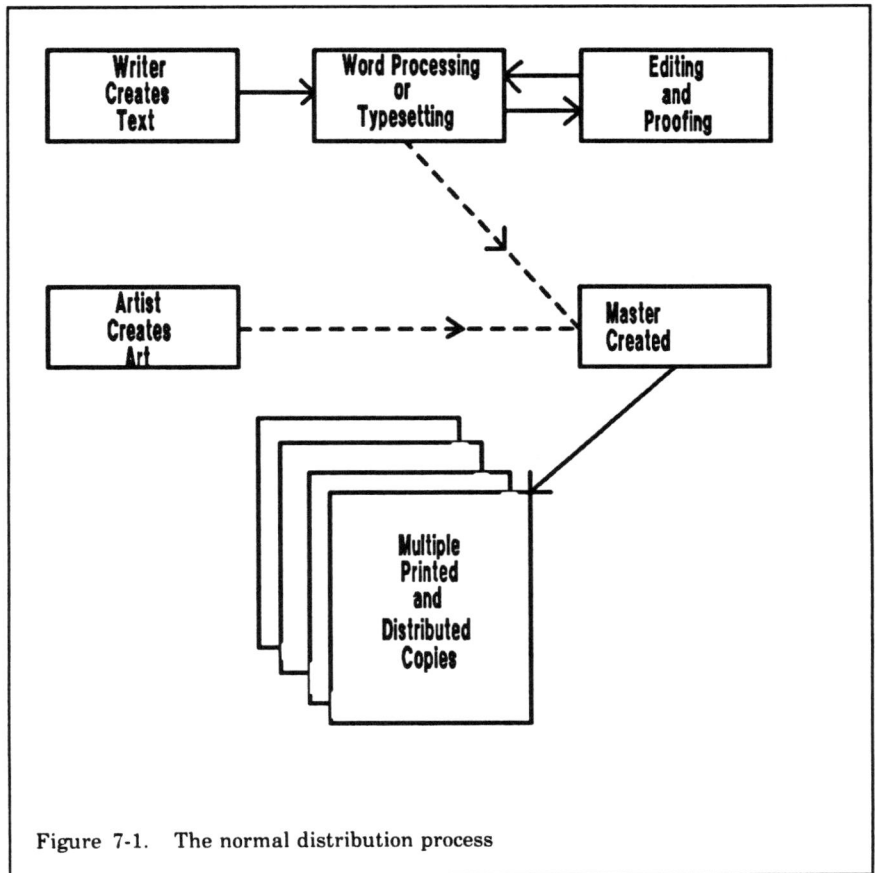

Figure 7-1. The normal distribution process

It is important to understand the magnitude of the task each time information is disseminated in your environment so that you can better understand how it is possible to provide better and more timely access to pertinent information in an on-line environment. Review *Evaluation Checklist* carefully to define your information access needs. The more care you take in this process, the easier it will be to create an on-line system that is best suited to your present and future information requirements.

Reducing Information Dissemination Costs

Every company environment needs ways to streamline the costs associated with doing business. The costs associated with getting information onto paper and then into the hands of the people who need that information may not be obvious.

Remember that for each piece of paper you place into someone's hand, there are many costs. The best way to understand these costs is to list the tasks required to make a document available for distribution:

- Create the text

- Print draft copies

- Review the text

- Approve the text

- Create the final master

- Produce copies

- Distribute the copies

- Integrate changed pages into existing documents or replace entire document

- Obsolete outdated copies

- Repeat the cycle to produce updates

Within each of these areas there are even more definable costs as you tally expenditures associated with personnel, equipment, materials, and training.

With an on-line text access system it is possible to significantly reduce the costs associated with the paper and staff required to place paper into the hands of the people who require the information. You can streamline the authoring and review process to reduce the costs associated with developing the text, and save on the costs of the paper and the costs associated with copying or printing. There are also savings on the staff required to prepare documents for distribution and the cost of the distribution.

What Do You Want from Your Text Access System? 99

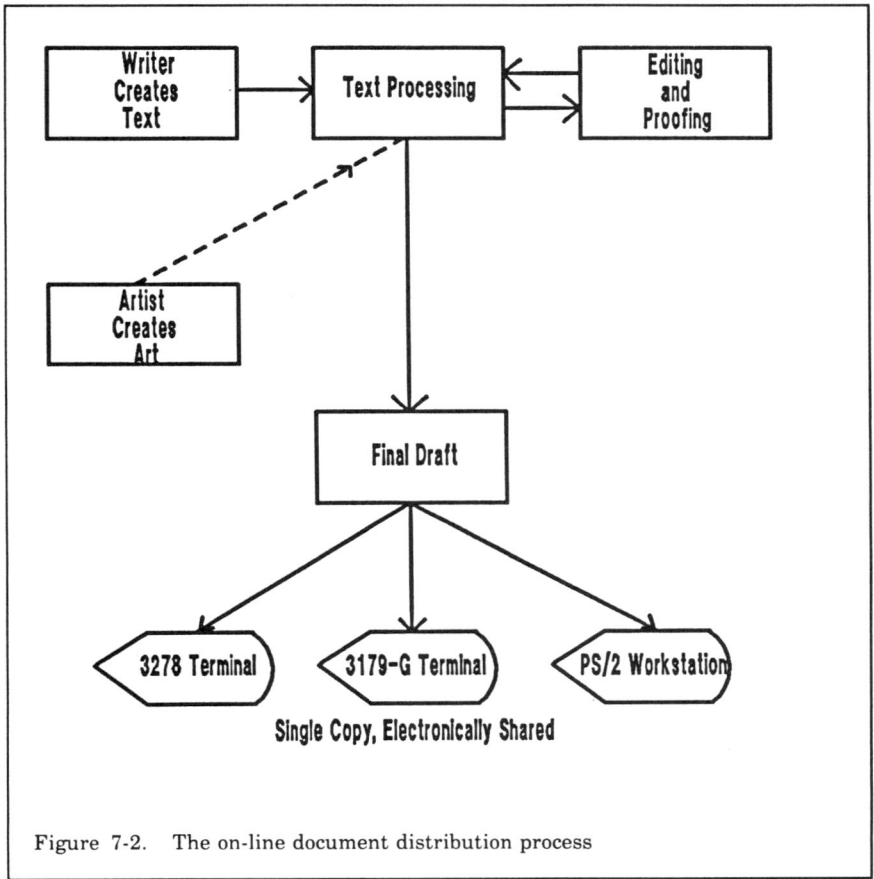

Figure 7-2. The on-line document distribution process

A quick review of your department or company-wide budget for printing and distribution may be enough to demonstrate the types of savings available.

The next section provides a checklist to help in your evaluation of your environment and your text access requirements.

Evaluation Checklist

To help you to use the balance of this book more effectively and to serve as a reference point for evaluating your information needs, we provide the following checklist. On first reading, it is intended to give you a baseline from which to evaluate your current environment. You must review your entire environment carefully to determine how a fully integrated on-line text management system can best fit into your corporate picture. We also hope this checklist will serve as a source of ideas for what is possible if you do not already have some thoughts as to what you would like to see implemented in your environment.

When you have completed your review of the checklist and determined what you would like to do, look at *WYSIWYG* on page 213 for some hints as to what directions your answers should be pointing.

1. **What are your publishing requirements?**

   - Memos/letters
   - Policy and procedures manuals for in-house distribution
   - Marketing material
   - User guides and reference materials associated with vendor products
   - User guides and reference materials created for use with products developed in-house
   - User guides and reference materials created for use with products developed for sale

2. **How much do you currently spend to create documents in-house?**

   Costs associated with:

   - Personnel
   - Developing drafts
   - Printing drafts and circulating for approval
   - Finalizing copy
   - Preparing masters for duplication
   - Duplication/printing/copying
   - Distribution

3. **Which publishing requirements would you like to satisfy with an on-line text application?**

   - Faster revision and distribution of documents
   - Increased availability of written material
   - Increased usability of written material
   - Less expensive distribution

4. **What type of text access best suits your environment?**

    - Application-based entry into a complex system of related text members
    - Context-sensitive entry into a complex system of related text members
    - Context-sensitive entry into a complex system of unrelated text members

5. **How sophisticated are your users?**
   Are they:

    - Afraid of the computer system?
    - People who will use only the functions necessary to do their own job?
    - Casual users of single applications?
    - Regular users of personal computing environments?
    - People who will use any system to its fullest?
    - People who enjoy learning and using new technology?

6. **Acceptable length of time for training users?**
   For those who are:

    - Afraid of the computer system: several months
    - People who will use only the functions necessary to do their own job: several weeks
    - Casual users of single applications: a week
    - Regular users of personal computing environments: a week
    - People who will use any system to its fullest: a few days
    - People who enjoy learning and using new technology: a few days

7. **What is your current MIS environment?**

    - In-house or service bureau?
    - Operating system?
        ∘ VM?
        ∘ MVS?
        ∘ VSE?
        ∘ A combination? If so, where does the text composition function normally reside?
    - How many applications do you currently use?
    - How much interactive computing does your shop provide?

- ° Very little?
- ° TSO or CMS?
- ° PCs also serving as mainframe terminals?
- How much of your current data processing resources are currently consumed?

8. **Are you restricted to using existing hardware, or can you purchase new hardware?**

   - No budget available
   - Budget requests must be made one year or more in advance
   - Money is made available based on demonstrated need
   - Purchases require approval from management more than one level higher

9. **Can your data processing resources be expanded?**

   - Processing resources
   - Storage
   - Terminals and displays

10. **How sophisticated is your hardware environment?**
    Do the end users have:

    - Monochrome displays?
    - Color displays?
    - Color displays with graphics capability?
    - High resolution color graphics displays?
    - Access to both PC and host-based programs?
    - Access to both PC and host from one workstation?
    - Access to information stored on-line, near-line, and off-line without intervention by a systems person?

11. **What type of terminals will users have?**

    - Monochrome displays attached only to the mainframe
    - Color displays attached only to the mainframe
    - Color displays with graphics capability attached only to the mainframe
    - High resolution color graphics displays attached only to the mainframe
    - Any of the above also attached to a PC or a LAN

12. **Will all users have their own terminals?**

- Each user has a personal terminal
- Users share terminal access within a work group

13. **What are your allowable development costs?**

    - Some percentage of existing revenues
    - Some percentage of projected revenues
    - Some percentage of anticipated savings
    - Flat dollar amount based on current estimating formulas

14. **What are your allowable operating expenses after completion?**

    - Some percentage of existing revenues
    - Some percentage of projected revenues
    - Some percentage of anticipated savings
    - Flat dollar amount based on current estimating formulas

15. **What is your allowable resource usage after completion?**

    - Support personnel
    - Maintenance personnel
    - CPU and DASD consumption

16. **What is the acceptable length of time for development and implementation?**

    - Less than one year: Consider purchasing a shell
    - One to two years
    - More than two years

17. **What is the acceptable length of time for training maintenance programmers?**

    - If the programmer was part of the project, no training time should be required
    - For a new programmer, assume at least two months

Part

3

Display Design

In this section we look carefully at the design questions that drive the development of the on-line text access, perusal, and management system you want to create. If you have never given a great amount of consideration to how text is displayed back to the screen or if you have not given serious consideration to all of the facilities, you might want to make available to the end users of your system, these chapters will provide a reference point for your design considerations.

Chapter

8

Designing Screen Text Appearance

Text does not appear on a terminal screen in the same format and manner in which it appears on paper. Formatting restrictions, screen size and color, and readability of the screen font(s) are just some of the factors you must take into account when designing screens for the presentation of on-line text. We begin with the restrictions, and follow that with a discussion of viewing strategies and formatting problems. This section concludes with an examination of the human interfaces necessary to access text in a terminal display environment.

Our treatment of the issues should provide you with enough information to create a viable on-line text display environment. For more information on screen design considerations, you may also want to check the following references:

- *Designing the User Interface*, Ben Shneiderman, Reading, MA, Addison-Wesley (1987).

- *Handbook of Screen Format Design*, Wilbert O. Galitz, Wellesley, MA, QED Information Sciences, Inc. (1985).

- *Common User Access Panel Design and User Interaction*, IBM Publication SC25-4351, IBM Corporation (1987).

Screen Environment Restrictions

Modern IBM mainframe displays suffer from several restrictions which must be taken into account when designing an on-line text perusal system. These restrictions involve:

- Color
- Mixed case
- Fonts and highlighting
- Screen depth

As you design an application to manage and provide on-line text, you must be aware of all the possible environments in which it may be used. Where possible, your system should automatically determine its terminal environment and adjust itself to optimize the characteristics of a particular terminal.

Model	Rows	Cols	Hiliting	Color	Graphics
3178-2	24	80	Normal	No	No
3179-2	24	80	Ext.	No	No
3179-G	32	80	Ext.	7	Yes
3180	43	80	Ext.	No	No
3192-2	24	80	Ext.	No	No
3192-G	32	80	Ext.	7	Yes
3193	43	80	Ext.	No	Image
3277	24	80	Normal	No	No
3278-2	24	80	Ext.	No	No
3278-5	24	132	Ext.	No	No
3279-2	24	80	Ext.	4	No
3279-3	32	80	Ext.	4	No
3279-3X	32	80	Ext.	4	Yes
3290	46	157	Ext.	No	Yes

Table 1.   IBM 3270-type terminals

Your IBM mainframe environment may include a large mix of terminal types and capabilities. These range from very old model 3277s which have only 24 lines of uppercase characters in green to PS/2s with 32 lines of scalable fonts on a high-resolution color monitor, as shown in Table 1. The common practice of designing down to the common denominator in such an environment is not a good tactic. It is much better to design your display manager so that it can make good use of any terminal capabilities available.

Color

The use of multiple colors to coordinate displays and direct attention is extremely important, but it can be overused. Multi-color displays are very useful for controlling and weighting the appearance of text and messages, but too many colors, colors that are too bright, or unappealing color combinations can detract and make unusable an otherwise well-designed text display.

Mixed Case

Studies of how people read have consistently shown that *mixed case* text, mixing upper- and lowercase characters, is easier to read, less tiring on the eyes, and understood more quickly.

Most IBM host-attached terminals now support mixed case, but you may find that your shop still has a few 3277s which have only an uppercase screen font. These terminals translate all lower case text coming to them into the uppercase equivalents. IBM 3278 terminals typically have a switch marked "A,a" on the top and "A" on the bottom. This switch controls whether the terminal performs the translation or not. Newer terminals, such as the 3179 and 3192, do not offer such a control. All text is displayed as coded.

You should require mixed case capability in the terminals on which your on-line text system is going to run. If the user can toggle the case feature as on 3278s, require that it be in mixed case mode for your system. Unfortunately, it is not possible for an application program to determine how the switch is set.

Fonts and Highlighting

Another aid to readability is the size of the screen font and if it is fixed-pitch or proportional. The ability to display text in a variety of type styles and sizes, using proportional screen fonts rather than fixed-pitch fonts, should be exploited if available. Readability and understandability can be dramatically improved by a judicious use of type styles.

IBM sells few terminal models which have the ability to display multiple fonts. You are typically limited to one screen font over which you may have highlighting control. Some workstations serving as 3270 emulators may have the ability to show fonts in different sizes. If you are designing and building your own system for text display, consider these workstations as possible display devices.

Highlighting can be used to improve readability in much the same way as multiple type styles. High intensity is the most common form of highlighting available. It cannot be used nearly as effectively as more sophisticated highlighting techniques, but if it is all you have, then use it where appropriate. Some good uses include serious attention-demanding messages and re-displays of screens with erroneous entries marked for quick detection. Judicious use of underlining and reverse video can also improve the readability and usability of a display text.

Using the ability to cause the text to blink should be avoided in text display except in short messages displayed while a long process is running. Here, the activity on the screen can give the impression of a faster response, sometimes a vital factor in user acceptance. The important thing to remember about highlighting is that *less is more*. If you use too much highlighting on a single screen, or use it too often, it loses its impact.

If you are building a HyperText system, you should mark the words or phrases that can be selected to activate links to other text. Any of these highlighting methods can be used, but the fewer you have to work with in your most common terminal environment, the harder it is to avoid overusing it or using it consistently.

Screen Depth

Most IBM 3270 type terminals still offer 24 lines of text on a screen. The terminals capable of graphics offer 32 lines, and the *image-only* terminal, the 3193, offers 43 lines. Some workstation terminal emulators can offer up to 50 lines. It is important to know what type of terminals your system will be running on to design the screen layouts appropriately. It is also important to design the text layout to take advantage of the screen sizes. This is discussed in more detail in *Just a Few More Questions* on page 161, but for now be aware that the amount of information that appears on a screen and the proportion of blank to filled space are important factors in how quickly and well the user will understand the information.

In on-line text environments you want to try and ensure that a complete topic or subtopic appears on each screen. *Screen transition*, moving from screen to screen while viewing the text, is a much more invasive and distracting process than page transition in a book. If the information you are presenting is too complex to fit on one display screen, it must be modularized into smaller subtopics.

If your system is operating with terminals with different characteristics, you may want to consider a system which dynamically reconfigures and perhaps recomposes to take advantage of terminals with deeper text space. Also, remember that you always lose a few lines to help information, screen and system titles, and other standard, non-changing text. This can dramatically reduce the amount of space on the screen for real information. As you look more carefully at your system design, consider a system that allows much of this static information to be removed from the screen.

Other Hardware Restrictions

Aside from screen depth, there are other hardware restrictions to be concerned about, particularly in a HyperText environment. You will want to be able to provide text or other information in windows within your text to some degree. Even if the only windowing you do is to provide configurable windows for static information that can be turned on and off, you will ultimately find that IBM terminals do not offer many aesthetic features for windowing. Unless you limit yourself to a graphics-capable display, you will be severely restricted on window borders, shapes, and sizes, although it is not impossible to do. Consider alternatives, such as non-IBM terminals and workstations that offer connectivity to IBM mainframes but still provide high resolution screens capable of handling complex graphics and multi-color screen image design.

Another restrictive area is scrolling. IBM 3270 architecture does not allow for continuous smooth scrolling of text in an economical manner. You must take this into account in your screen design.

It is possible to scroll a 3270 type screen only one character or line at a time, but to do so repeatedly requires two things:

- The user must press a program function (PF), program attention (PA) or ENTER key for each scroll.

- The system must process an I/O operation for each scroll.

Presenting I/O interrupts to an IBM mainframe is an expensive process which many users pay for in dollars. Consequently, smooth scrolling is seldom implemented on real-world mainframe systems.

Since there is no repeat on 3270 PF keys, there is little call for single line scrolling. The user's finger tires too quickly.

It is certainly possible to display a file scrolling one line at a time across a screen and each previous line moving up as it goes, but each new line displayed represents another I/O operation and another cost to the user. The 3270 architecture is simply not intended to handle display operations in that manner.

A similar restriction exists concerning *hot keys*. IBM terminals do not allow for any key to be set up to trigger an interrupt to the current process. Such keys must be programmed around the function (PF) and program attention (PA) keys. Even when these are used, the supporting software or operating system may not allow them to serve as interrupt keys, but only as function keys to use in place of the **ENTER** key.

Chapter

9

Formatting the Presentation

Another factor you need to consider when designing the appearance of text on the screen is how that information is formatted. Formatting is the task of massaging the raw text into a form in which it is visually readable and in which it conveys information in *chunks*. We will explore several aspects of this task: These are:

- How does text that is not yet machine-readable enter the on-line system?

- How does existing machine readable text enter the on-line system?

- Where and how is it formatted?

- What are the maintenance problems with respect to formatting?

- What are the considerations for the physical display unit?

- What are the human factor considerations for the display methodology?

Capturing Text

Perhaps the largest problem with setting up any on-line text system is presented by the task of capturing the text to be displayed. This problem is not reduced by the fact that the text is to be displayed on a mainframe, but it may be simplified by the limitations of the display device to be used. There are several typical sources for the text:

- Re-keyed versions of paper documents
- Electronic documents copied into on-line text files
- Scanned printed documents into on-line text files

Keying

In building an on-line text system, it is most convenient if the documents to be displayed are already available in a machine-readable form, stored somewhere on your host computer system. There are always those documents, however, which must be manually keyed from pre-printed, typeset, or typed paper documents directly into your host environment.

If most of the documents you need on-line currently exist only in paper form (typed or typeset), then you may have to start building your on-line text database by manually keying these documents into the on-line file system. Manual keying is also the technique of choice for creating new documents in the on-line system.

Maintenance of keyed copies of paper documents can become a problem if you continue to use manual updating techniques for the paper documents. As the documents change over time, one of two things happens:

- The electronic version of a typeset document becomes out of date as the manual updates to the original are applied.

- You encounter a double maintenance problem by having to manually update the typeset document, then apply the same updates to the on-line version by editing it.

The solution is to make the typeset document an electronic one. Perform all updates to the on-line version of the document, then create a new master for typesetting. If you use one of the host composition systems that can produce an electronic file readable by your typesetting system, you can reduce most of the work involved with creating the typeset masters. Alternatively, you might choose to bypass typesetting altogether and move into demand electronic publishing.[1] This provides the added benefit of migrating more of your document processing into an electronic arena, although you may encounter resistance from document designers who have been updating typeset documents in the more traditional manner.

Copying

You may already have a large collection of documents available as machine readable files within your computer system. These are the documents that you routinely print and that form a rich source of on-line text material. Copying text from these documents, either before or during composition of the text, helps to ensure synchronization between the printed and on-line material.

Merely copying text blocks into new files does pose a maintenance problem, however. What is needed is a technique that uses a single text source for both printed and on-line material, recreating both each time the source is updated. There are a couple of ways to do this:

- **A single source file can be composed for different formats using a sophisticated composition program, such as IBM's Document Composition Facility (DCF).**

  DCF, and other host-based composition systems like it, use profiles and macro libraries to control the formatting of the document. Using one profile, DCF can compose the document for printing on a laser printer. Using a different profile, DCF can compose the same source document for the on-line browsing system. The same macro libraries should be used for both environments.

  The differences in the two environments can be limited to the format, with the same text formatted for on-line display or for

---

[1] See P. C. McGrew and W. D. McDaniel, *In-House Publishing in a Mainframe Environment*, New York: McGraw-Hill, Revised 1989.

printing, or it can extend to the selection of totally different text for each environment.

- **A separate, on-line text preparation program can be used to extract the on-line text from either the original source file or the output file that has been composed for printing.**

An on-line text preparation program would have to read the source documents, interpreting whatever text processing markup they contained, and then extract appropriate text for the on-line system. To do this it would be necessary for the extraction program to understand all of the markup used in formatting the printed document. Writing such a program would be virtually identical to re-creating the formatter used for producing the printed version. This is how existing on-line text display products, such as Goal Systems *Preference*, import files into a free-standing text display environment which is independent of the source used for composing the printed version of the document.

A slightly simpler task is the creation of an extraction program for post-processing the composed text. This program does not have to interpret markup language, but could be made to determine appropriate formatting for the on-line system. Such a program would be just an extraction program and its output would, most probably, have to be manually edited into the proper format for on-line display.

Scanning

Scanning printed documents into an on-line text system works only if you can live with the limitations. Most scanners produce graphic images of documents called *bitmaps*. These are rectangular arrays of black and white dots which, when displayed on a graphics terminal, reproduce an image of the scanned document. This image is useless to an on-line text system unless the displays you use can effectively handle graphic (especially bitmapped) images. Most IBM mainframe terminal models cannot, and those that do are not very efficient.

Even if the terminals in your system could support the image display, using bit images for on-line text removes the possibility of searching the text for character strings entered by the user.

Some scanners have the ability to perform Optical Character Recognition (OCR). OCR is a process of recognizing and extracting characters from the scanned image. This provides you with coded text, in ASCII or EBCDIC, that can be placed into your on-line text database.

No OCR process is completely accurate, however. All scanners have limitations, some quite severe, which limit the usability of this technique. Most OCR scanners can recognize only a limited number of fonts, often only fixed-pitch, typewriter fonts. Some cannot recognize font changes on a single line, even if they can recognize heading fonts versus text fonts. Scanners also confuse letters like *D* and *O*, which necessitates intensive proofing and correction by a human proofreader after the scan. This extra effort is often significant enough to make full re-keying of the text a viable alternative. See *Scanning* on page 156 for more information on evaluating scanning as a text capture technique for your environment.

Formatting the Text

Just as text on a page must be formatted or composed for printing, so must text for on-line presentation. Formatting is critical for on-line text because the medium, particularly on IBM mainframes, is so limited. The screen size is limited, the font is typically fixed-pitch, and there are usually limited highlighting capabilities. These factors all combine to make on-line text formatting one of the most important aspects of any text system.

There are four main techniques that can be used for formatting text for on-line display. These are:

- Manually formatting the text into static display files or *panels* of fixed width and depth, as shown in Figure 9-1 on page 120

```
TUTORIAL ---------------- INTRODUCTION (CONTINUED) ------------------ TUTORIAL
COMMAND --->
                                                   DEFAULT ARRANGEMENT
                                                    FOR PF KEY PAD
You may use the following program function (PF)  |--------|--------|--------|
keys while viewing the tutorial:                 |  HELP  |        |  END   |
                                                 | PF1 or |        | PF3 or |
                                                 |  PF13  |        |  PF15  |
    HELP  - to get help on how to use the tutorial. |--------|--------|--------|
    END   - to end the tutorial.                 |        |        |        |
    UP    - to display a higher level list of topics.|    |        |        |
    DOWN  - to go on to the next topic (skip).   |        |        |        |
    LEFT  - to display the previous page (back). |--------|--------|--------|
    RIGHT - to display the next page, which is   |   UP   |  DOWN  |        |
            the same as pressing ENTER.          | PF7 or | PF8 or |        |
                                                 |  PF19  |  PF20  |        |
                                                 |--------|--------|--------|
                                                 |  LEFT  | RIGHT  |        |
                                                 |PF10 or |PF11 or |        |
                                                 |  PF22  |  PF23  |        |
                                                 |--------|--------|--------|
```

Figure 9-1. A common 3270-type screen panel

- Using a composition system to compose the text into static files, as described above

- Formatting the text for print, then using a program to display the text in a WYSIWYG manner, as shown in Figure 9-2 on page 121

Formatting the Presentation 121

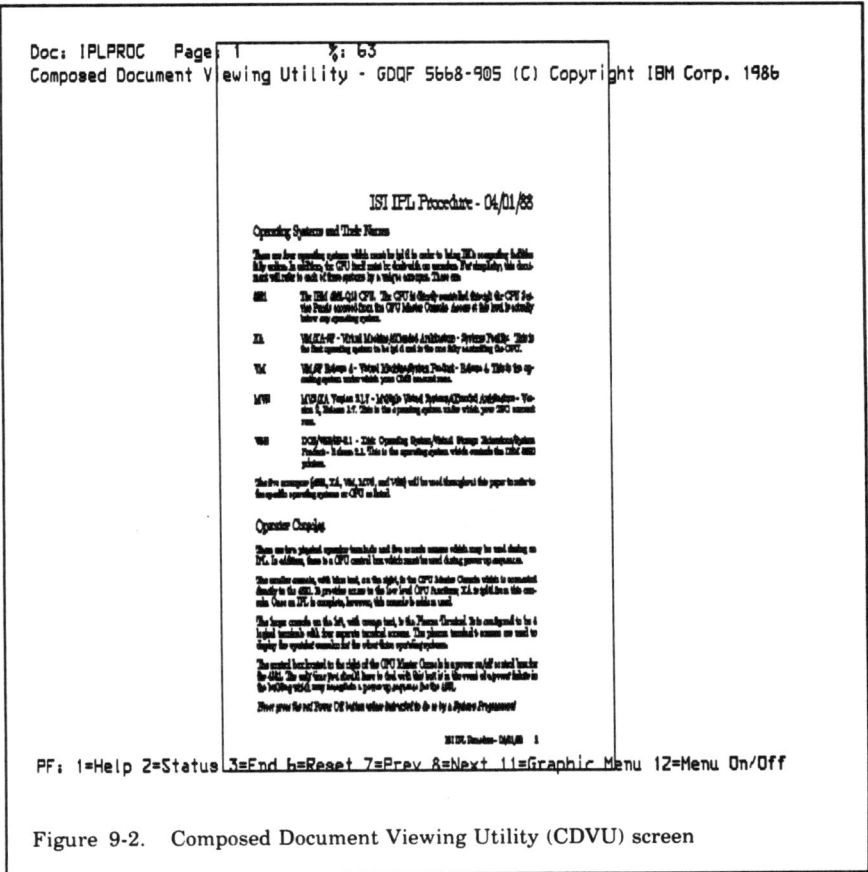

Figure 9-2. Composed Document Viewing Utility (CDVU) screen

- Formatting the text for variable sized *windows* on the screen, as shown in Figure 9-3 on page 122

```
                       HyperText Research Project
+-------------------------------------------------+    +---------------+
| HyperDoc: IPLPROC                               |    |     Help      |
|                                                 |    | PF1 - Help    |
|                                                 |    | PF2 - Links   |
| GSI IPL Procedure - 04/01/88                    |    | PF3 - Quit    |
|                                                 |    | PF4 - Bk 1/2  |
| Operating Systems and Their Names               |    | PF5 - Fd 1/2  |
| There are  four operating systems which must    |    | PF6 - Locate  |
| be IPL'd in order to  bring  GSI's computing    |    | PF7 - Back    |
| facilities fully online. In addition, the CPU   |    | PF8 - Frwd    |
| itself  must  be  dealt with on occasion. For   |    | PF10- First   |
| simplicity, this document will refer to  each   |    | PF11- Last    |
| of  these  systems by a unique acronym. These   |    | PF12- Level1  |
| Level: 1                      Line: 1 of 656    |    | ENT - Close   |
+-------------------------------------------------+    +---------------+
```

Figure 9-3. Windows on a screen: In this example there are two open windows on the screen. The text in the left screen has been formatted for the width and depth of the window.

Once you have established the formatting methodology to use, you must arrive at a viable maintenance philosophy. Maintaining the text, correcting and revising it, remains an issue long after the on-line text system is displaying it for all to see. Maintenance issues may even increase. How such maintenance affects the formatting of your text is an important consideration.

The effect of maintenance on displayed text depends on the display methodology used. In each case there are strengths and weaknesses to the display technique. Unfortunately, the advantages of a display technique are often at cross purposes with maintenance.

Manual Formatting

Manual formatting involves keying the text in exactly as it will display on the screen. This is a tedious process. In addition, you must make all of the decisions about heading and paragraph formatting and spacing each time you encounter the requirement in your text, which can lead to inconsistent formatting. It is very difficult to remain consistent with the number of lines you space down or the number of columns you indent.

Manual formatting can be a serious detriment to maintenance as well. Consider the effort involved in altering the look of any documentation globally, across your entire document database. For instance, imagine the manpower required if you have been manually formatting for 80-column, 24-line panels, but now wish to reformat for 32-line terminals because your shop is upgrading. You are going to spend a lot of time reformatting. With any significant number of documents in your text database, this proves to be a monumental task, probably monumental enough to ensure it is never accomplished.

Maintaining Manually Formatted Text This is certainly easy to change, but can be the most difficult to maintain if you also want a consistent appearance. Most manually formatted text is entered with a ragged right edge. While this makes the addition or deletion of a single word easy, a simple change of phrasing can alter several lines of text, each requiring manual editing. The problem becomes worse if your text contains its own running headings and footings.

Composing Text

Using a composition system to format the text for display is a *much* better way to format your on-line text than manually keying it. Using a composition system, such as DCF, assures consistency of formatting and allows global format changes to be made much more efficiently. With a composition system that uses formatting profiles or style specification files, you simply re-define the profile and recompose the documents to alter the formatting and appearance.

Typical composition systems allow the definition of running headings and footings that delimit the pages explicitly. This lends itself to static panels of fixed width and depth that either fill the screen or leave a small area for instructions and help information.

Maintaining Composed Text If your source text is marked up in a composition language and can be re-composed, you are probably in the best situation. The changes can be made using any convenient editor, re-composed with new line endings, and be available for access in a fairly short time. The trouble with this approach, however, is that the pagination and flow of the document that displayed nicely once may change such that the flow is destroyed. If the document was composed into well-organized panels of on-line information, changing it and indiscriminately re-formatting the text may leave you with a hodge-podge mixture of half-panels and *orphaned* titles. The only solution is to have someone assigned to review the look of the presentation after all updates are made so that modifications can be made as needed before releasing the new version to the production environment.

Viewing Graphically Composed Text

Another formatting strategy is to use the text as composed for printing, but display it in a WYSIWYG manner on a mainframe terminal. This technique has several drawbacks. First, the only terminals that can be used are the more expensive graphics devices: IBM's 3179-G or 3192-G, for instance. There is also a much larger cost, at least in terms of CPU utilization, associated with displaying text in this manner. Graphics programs that scale and format such text are CPU-intensive. Finally, the process is inherently slow on most IBM mainframes.

The existing IBM products that can display a document composed for an IBM laser printer are the BrowseMaster component of the Publishing SolutionPac or the Graphics Display and Query Facility (GDQF) Composed Document Viewing Utility (CDVU) component. BrowseMaster is simply a repackaging of the older CDVU product, so their functionality and interfaces are the same. Each interprets an IBM Advanced Function Printing Data Stream (AFPDS) coded document, then scales and draws each character on a page as a set of vectors. This process can take over a minute for a complex page on a CPU carrying an average load.

The entire page can usually fit on the screen only at a 60% magnification, which makes fonts below 10 points in size unreadable. CDVU is generally not considered usable for true on-line text applications. It is an acceptable preview facility, particularly to check the visual organization of a document, but it is unusable for general document perusal. To be fair, it was never meant for that use.

Viewing the actual composed print file would have some distinct advantages if the issues of CPU utilization, time, and screen resolution could be resolved. You could keep composition at a one-step process, and only one output file would have to be kept. Multiple readers, some reading the printed version and others the on-line version, would be able to reference the same page and line breaks. Unfortunately, at this time the hardware technology has simply not caught up with the need.

Maintaining Graphically Formatted Text The same problems that arise with composed text are present if you are using a display program like IBM's BrowseMaster to view the text. If you have not carefully addressed pagination issues, the smooth flow of the document is destroyed. This can be more costly in a graphical display environment because of the added CPU overhead of the display technology.

Formatting for Windows

The window interface has become very popular in recent years, but is only now making its appearance in the mainframe world. Again, the problem has been a lack of power and flexibility in the IBM mainframe display architecture. While the architecture remains essentially unchanged, there is now enough programming flexibility to offer window interfaces for viewing text.

With a window interface available, the question of how the text is to be formatted for the windows quickly arises.

Should the window dimensions be controlled by the user? Should the text be allowed to overflow the window width, forcing readers to scroll?

What about text and window depth? Does the window depth have to be such that text is always displayed on discrete page boundaries? What happens if the window depth changes?

The designer of each system must answer each of these questions separately, based on known requirements and desires. We do, however, offer some suggestions.

Scrolling in Windows Scrolling on an IBM 3270 type terminal is often implemented as a full or half screen at a time operation. Since the 3270 display device architecture does not support a *hot key* facility, there is no facility for smoothly scrolling the text a line at a time as there is on a PC. Scrolling of text is a separate I/O operation, subject to response time issues just like any other operation. It is possible to implement scrolling as a line-at-a-time operation, and, if response time is very good, some impression of smooth scrolling results. This is a very CPU-intensive technique, however, and generally not acceptable due to the CPU cost and the response time demands.

This means that you should avoid left to right scrolling, if possible. Format text and windows so that full lines always appear. The window width is then static since there is no use in expanding the window beyond the text boundary.

The composed page depth is typically evident by the presence of running footings and headings. If the window in which you present the text does not match the page depth as indicated by these headings and footings, your text display appears confusing; the pages seem to float up or down the window as the reader scrolls through the on-line document. Page depth can be eliminated as a display issue by removing running footings and headings from the text. These can be built dynamically as part of the window. This actually gives you more control over the appearance of the document and can be quite useful.

```
                    HyperText Research Project
+-------------------------------------------------+    +---------------+
| HyperDoc: IPLPROC                               |    |     Help      |
|                                                 |    | PF1 - Help    |
|                                                 |    | PF2 - Links   |
| Navigating the Plasma Terminal                  |    | PF3 - Quit    |
| The Plasma Terminal is configured to present    |    | PF4 - Bk 1/2  |
| 4 3270 terminal sessions simultaneously. Each   |    | PF5 - Fd 1/2  |
| screen is a separate session and nothing on     |    | PF6 - Locate  |
| one screen is directly related to anything on   |    | PF7 - Back    |
| another. The screen with the cursor is the      |    | PF8 - Frwd    |
| active screen and the cursor must be "jumped"   |    | PF10- First   |
| from screen to screen to change the active      |    | PF11- Last    |
| session.                                        |    | PF12- Level1  |
| Level: 1              Line: 81 of 656           |    | ENT - Close   |
+-------------------------------------------------+    +---------------+
```

Figure 9-4. An example of scrolling within windows—part 1: Note the bottom line of the left window indicates that the first displayed line in the window is line 81 of the 656 line file. The next figure shows the same screen environment after scrolling forward 10 lines.

Without footings and headings, the text appears as a long galley, viewed through a window. This allows window depth to be variable, controlled by the user, and minimizes scrolling since no space in the window need be spent on distinguishing headings and footings. Footnotes can pose a problem, however, if they are designed to appear at the bottom of pages. For this, a HyperText interface may be the best solution, so that you can place footnotes at a separate location in the document and link them to their references.

Maintaining Text Formatted for Windows If you have chosen a window display methodology and are using a composition system to format the text for the windows, you have the best of all worlds. Because pages have essentially been eliminated in the window approach described above, there is less concern about the flow of the text. If a heading is orphaned—that is left at the bottom of a window with no text following it—the window size can be altered to display either less or more text at this point, forcing the flow back into shape.

If your text is manually formatted, but viewed through windows, you still have some of the problems associated with manually formatted text, but, again, the flow of the document is as much under the control of the display technology as it is the formatter. This should allow you a lot of flexibility in editing the text.

Who Is in Control?

Given the trade-offs between formatting methodologies, human factors, and readability issues, it is natural to ask what aspect of the design should take precedence. Does the formatting drive how the information is displayed, or does the display mechanism drive how the information is formatted? The answer, as usual, is "a little bit of both."

As a guideline, the needs of the information should, as much as possible, drive how the information is presented and displayed. You should not settle for an unusable and unreadable display of text due to characteristics of the display hardware or software. It is more important that the information be presented so that it can be navigated easily and read so that its information content comes through readily. Changes to the text should not be allowed to corrupt the

```
                    HyperText Research Project
     +--------------------------------------------+    +---------------+
     | HyperDoc: IPLPROC                          |    |      Help     |
     |                                            |    | PF1 - Help    |
     |                                            |    | PF2 - Links   |
     |       To jump from logical terminal to logical |    | PF3 - Quit    |
     | terminal  on the Plasma Terminal, you use the  |    | PF4 - Bk 1/2  |
     | Jump Screen key. This  is  the  Alternate-PA3  |    | PF5 - Fd 1/2  |
     | key.  PA3  is located in the upper right area  |    | PF6 - Locate  |
     | of  the  keyboard;  there  is  an  ALT key on  |    | PF7 - Back    |
     | either side of the space bar.  Press and hold  |    | PF8 - Frwd    |
     | the ALT key while pressing the PA3/JmpSc key.  |    | PF10- First   |
     | The cursor will jump from one quadrant of the  |    | PF11- Last    |
     | screen to the next in a  clockwise  rotation.  |    | PF12- Level1  |
     | Level: 1                    Line: 91 of 656   |    | ENT - Close   |
     +--------------------------------------------+    +---------------+
```

Figure 9-5. The window after one scrolling operation

flow and logical partitioning of the text simply because it is displayed on a terminal.

The last time we checked, however, we were all in a real world with real limitations on technology and budgets. It may not always be possible to have WYSIWYG terminals for all of our text display needs. Some people may have to get by with 24-line rather than 32-line terminals. Some other person may have the only 132 by 43-line terminal in the shop, but still have a real need to view on-line documentation. It is the system designer's job to integrate these different and often conflicting displays with the overall system formatting philosophy in order to provide the greatest service with the least degradation in quality and usability.

A proper formatting methodology, chosen for its applicability and usability, with an eye toward simple, non-disruptive text maintenance can allow the needs of the text to control the presentation while compromising favorably with the demands of the display mechanism.

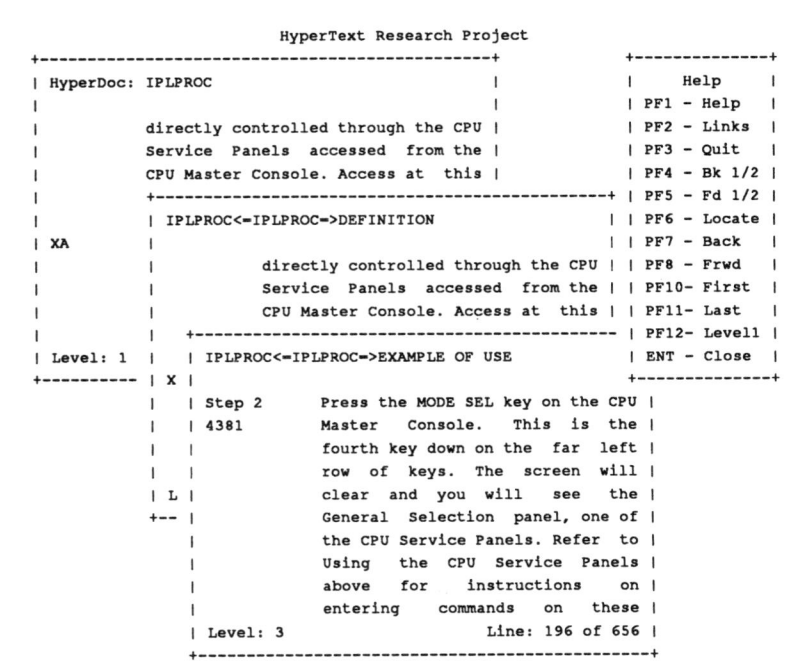

Figure 9-6. An example of text formatted for windows: In this illustration there are four windows open: the help window and three text windows. The text is formatted for the window size. If the formatting changes, corresponding changes may be necessary to the window programs.

Consistency

This issue of flow is important. It is vital that your on-line displays continue to look the same after editing as they did before so that readers are not distracted from using the text as a tool. Inconsistent formatting brought on by a lack of control during the maintenance process can disrupt the usability of an otherwise well-thought-out on-line text perusal system.

In the next section, we discuss one particular design decision which has a large effect on the formatting and display issues discussed here: the question of whether to use full-screen panels or windows.

Chapter

10

Presentation Control

Presentation control is concerned with how text is presented to readers and how they navigate and interact with the displayed text. In this section we examine the two main display philosophies, panels and windows, and the interaction issues common to these display strategies.

A debate between devotees of window presentation environments and those who favor full panels of text has been raging for several years. Nowhere has the debate been greater than in the IBM mainframe world, where most terminals do not have the graphics support to allow highly dynamic, sophisticated window-based applications. For many years terminals attached to IBM mainframes have had only one color and one font. This is still true for many large mainframe users. As a result, the advocates of full-screen panels have always held the high ground in the debate. This dominance seems to be changing with the introduction of IBM's Systems Application Architecture (SAA), which advocates that user presentation should be handled with a window environment, such as those available in the OS/2 Presentation Manager. No one has yet clearly stated how mainframe users are going to see windows as sophisticated as those that are common for PC, PS/2, and Macintosh users, but the statement of direction has been made by IBM.

We do *not* consider a full-screen panel display to be a special case of a single, full-screen window. Panels of information and windows of information represent two distinctly different text presentation philosophies. We explore both in some detail to arrive at scenarios where each is appropriate.

What Are Windows?

If only from TV commercials on Super Bowl Sunday, almost everyone associated with interactive computing has heard of *windows*. Window interfaces have popped up in everything from personal computers and video games to automobile dashboards. The reason they have become so ubiquitous is that windows are easy to understand and easy to use.

Window interfaces present information and interaction in small, rectangular pieces of screen real estate. They have emerged as one of the most significant advances in information presentation technology. Window interface systems allow users to see information presented in a well-organized, partitioned manner. New information is not lost within previously displayed data because the context in which the new information was requested or derived is maintained.

Beyond information presentation, windows allow interaction to be partitioned as well. Using pointing devices such as mice or moving the screen cursor from window to window allows the user to change context automatically. This allows users more opportunity to associate syntax with semantics when interacting with a system.

Window environments are not always appropriate vehicles for text display, however. Such environments depend heavily on a display that offers many options. To make the windows do their job at the visual and cognitive level, the display must allow a designer to visually identify several window components:

- The window outline

- An action or menu bar

- Scroll bars, if necessary

- The application display area

The display options to provide the necessary variety for these window components can consist of several things, depending on the display technology available:

- Color

- Highlighted text, reverse video, or underlining

- Graphic *icons* representing processes or commands

- Programmable cursor shapes

If the display does not offer sufficient variety in its options, a window interface can appear cluttered, disorganized, and be very difficult to use.

What Are Panels?

Full-screen *panels* are the more traditional interaction screens for IBM host-based applications. A panel can, to some degree, be thought of as a single window filling the screen. A hierarchy of panels can be thought of as a set of windows covering each other completely. This view is deceptively simple, however, and we have already said that we do not consider a panel interface to be a special, trivial case of a windowed environment.

Panel interfaces, as we have grown used to them on mainframe systems, may offer a variety of one-word programmed function key definitions, but do not offer anything truly comparable to a generic menu bar or scroll bars. Interactions may require only a single keystroke, but the context of that keystroke does not usually change based on cursor location.

Panels do not depend on the display capability of the terminal as much as window interfaces do. Color and highlighting can be very useful in panel design, but since each panel is a self-contained unit of work, it is not as necessary to visually separate each function as it is with window interfaces. If semantic separation is needed, the application simply switches to another panel, often carrying significant information from one panel to another.

Panel interfaces are much simpler to develop than windows for many reasons:

- Program function key and command semantics remain constant on a given panel

- There is no problem of placement; every panel covers the screen

- Scrolling can usually be eliminated.

Windows versus Panels

It is now time to seriously evaluate your application to determine which presentation method is most appropriate. We ask the following questions:

- When are windows or panels appropriate?

- What are the advantages and disadvantages of each presentation strategy?

- What are appropriate viewing methods for windows and panels?

- What are the considerations in deciding on tiled or overlapping windows?

These are all questions that must be evaluated by the system designer. The designer of an on-line text system must decide how the system is to be used and provide tools and features to guide the user in that usage. If the system does not provide such guidance, usage patterns become erratic, confusing, and frustrating.

This is not to say that only one usage path should be provided. A system as free form as a text display facility should offer many alternatives and variations for use. Each should be intentionally designed and implemented by the designer, however, and not left to chance. Inappropriate and difficult usage patterns should be eliminated by design so that it is actually more difficult to use the system in an inappropriate manner than it is to choose one of the appropriate pathways.

The advantages of windows are most evident when you consider the information *chunking* principle. Recent psychological and psychometric studies have indicated that people react better to information when it is presented in small, digestible chunks that are somehow complete in and of themselves. A good discussion of the concepts can be found in *The IBM Systems Journal*, Vol. 27, No. 3 (1988) in the several articles dealing with IBM's *Common User Access* (CUA) component of its recently announced *Systems Application Architecture* (SAA).

The visual partitioning of information by the presence of window borders has been determined to be another major benefit of window environments. The borders separate the information packets into digestible pieces that maintain a relationship with each other in the reader's mind.

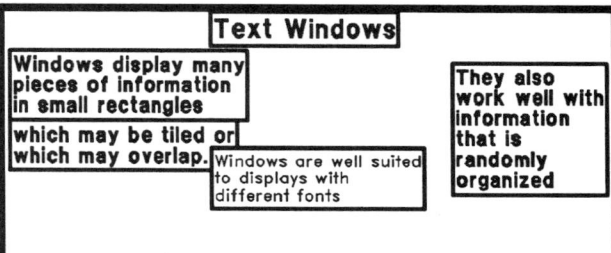

Figure 10-1. Panel presentation versus window presentation

Windows have disadvantages, however, particularly on terminals with a single fixed-size font such as IBM 3270s. The biggest problem is that windows eat up screen space in borders and menu or scroll bars reducing the amount of information available on a single screen. In addition, the non-scalable font means that you cannot have small windows with a lot of information in them. Typically, a window on a 3270 screen should not be much smaller than 30–50 characters in width and at least 5–10 lines deep. This averages out to about one-fourth of the screen occupied for each window. If they are smaller, not enough information can be presented. Larger windows mean that you do not have enough screen real estate to do

```
                         HyperText Research Project
      +------------------------------------------------+  +---------------+
      | HyperDoc: IPLPROC                              |  |      Help     |
      |                                                |  | PF1  - Help   |
      |           directly controlled through the CPU  |  | PF2  - Links  |
      |           Service Panels accessed from the     |  | PF3  - Quit   |
      |           CPU Master Console. Access at this   |  | PF4  - Bk 1/2 |
      |           +------------------------------------------+ PF5 - Fd 1/2 |
      |           | IPLPROC<-IPLPROC->DEFINITION       |  | PF6  - Locate |
      | XA        |                                    |  | PF7  - Back   |
      |           |           directly controlled through the CPU | PF8 - Frwd |
      |           |           Service Panels accessed from the    | PF10- First |
      |           |           CPU Master Console. Access at this  | PF11- Last  |
      |           |           +------------------------------------------+ PF12 - Level1 |
      | Level: 1  |           | IPLPROC<-IPLPROC->EXAMPLE OF USE    | ENT - Close |
      +---------- | X |                                             +---------------+
                  |           | Step 3        Press the MODE SEL key on the CPU |
                  |           | 4381          Master Console. This is the      |
                  |           |               fourth key down on the far left  |
                  |           |               row of keys. The screen will     |
                  | L |                       clear and you will see the       |
                  +-- |                       General Selection panel, one of  |
                      |                       the CPU Service Panels. Refer to |
                      |                       Using the CPU Service Panels     |
                      |                       above for instructions on        |
                      |                       entering commands on these       |
                      | Level: 3                        Line: 196 of 656       |
                      +-------------------------------------------------+
```

Figure 10-2. Overlapping windows: We have used this illustration already to show formatted text within windows, but it also provides a good example of the continuity of path possible in a window display environment.

more than one or two windows, so you might as well go to full- or half-screen panels.

Another drawback to windows is that they require much more complex driver software than panels. Windows must be sized, positioned, filled, then drawn. Full panels need only to be filled and displayed.

Panels are easier to design and build than windows, but care must be taken to provide a track of the panel hierarchy for the user. This aids in system navigation. The best way to implement a panel interface is to have each panel designated by a sequence of numbers that place it on the hierarchical tree. The number 3.0 indicates that this is a primary panel at level three. It accesses 3.1 or 3.2, which are second-level panels. From 3.1 we can access 3.1.1, 3.1.2, or 3.1.3 and so on.

This numeration hierarchy works, but if the designer lets the hierarchy become too deep, it quickly becomes cumbersome to read and understand. In addition, panel numbering does not lend itself well to lateral movement or tracking that movement through a system. If you can access panel 4.1.3.5.4.2 from panel 3.8.2.6.4.3, the numbering appears awkward and there is little instinctive knowledge of the starting point. Panel designers should avoid such deep trees of panels and provide tools for more lateral movement through the hierarchy in order to enhance the usability of their system.

Certainly, with panels, it is easier to adhere to the rule that each *chunk* of information should appear on a single screen. Panels are larger and offer more space to operate in. They also allow you to design in much more white space, which has been shown to make a document more readable.

Conversely, windows offer the ability to add small amounts of related information in a context-preserving manner. Windows can also be arranged on the screen so that most, if not all, of the entire path remains visible to the reader.

Selecting the Appropriate Presentation Method

Windows provide small *slices* of information, temporally preserve context by floating the newest information to the top of the display stack, and can be spatially organized to represent relations between informational *chunks*. Typically, a window does not provide all of the text on a topic. It usually provides associative or visual links to other information chunks that can be displayed in other windows.

Panels provide full *pages* of information, each page standing alone in context. Panels can be hierarchically organized, but be sure the organization is made visually apparent in some manner. While panels may contain pointers to other information, each panel is usually complete with respect to the information it attempts to present.

Choosing the appropriate display strategy should be a process of deciding how the information to be presented is organized and how it can best be presented to the user.

Is it already *chunked*? Does it need temporal context to be understood? How many other chunks does a typical slice of text reference or point to? If this number is very high, windows are probably a better presentation strategy than panels.

Is the information already organized into large, complete pages, with few references to other text? Is the amount of information in each chunk so high that it would not display well in a small window? In these instances panels may be the better strategy.

Finally, can the organization of the information be made visually apparent to the user using panels? If not, strongly consider using the window paradigm. Alternatively, if the organization is essentially linear, then panels are a better display technique.

Windows: Tiling or Overlapping?

One last topic with respect to windows alone is that of placement. There are two distinct window placement philosophies:

- Tiling windows

- Overlapping windows

Tiling Windows

Tiling windows is the process of partitioning the screen space into a set of non-overlapping rectangles, as shown in Figure 10-3 on page 139. If one window is moved or resized, the others are shifted and resized to ensure that there is no overlapping. Tiled window systems are often more static, with fixed and dedicated windows.

In tiled systems the user can deal with only five to seven windows before they become lost in the screen environment. Tiled windows should not all be the same size and shape, and only a few should be square. The eye reads text from rectangular spaces more easily than from square spaces. Varying the size of tiled windows provides visual clues as to the purpose of the window and aids differentiation of the windows. This same advantage presents some challenges to formatting text for display in those windows.

```
                         HyperText Research Project
+-----------------------------------------------+     +---------------+
| HyperDoc: IPLPROC                             |     |      Help     |
|                                               |     | PF1 - Help    |
|            directly controlled through the CPU|     | PF2 - Links   |
|            Service Panels accessed from the   |     | PF3 - Quit    |
|            CPU Master Console. Access at this |     | PF4 - Bk 1/2  |
|            level is actually below any        |     | PF5 - Fd 1/2  |
|            operating system.                  |     | PF6 - Locate  |
| XA         VM/XA-SF - Virtual Machine/eXtended|     | PF7 - Back    |
|            Architecture - Systems Facility.   |     | PF8 - Frwd    |
|            This is the first operating system |     | PF10- First   |
|                                               |     | PF11- Last    |
|            to be ipl'd and is the one fully   |     | PF12- Level1  |
| Level: 1                      Line: 13 of 656 |     | ENT - Close   |
+--------------+--------------------------------+-----+---------------+
               | IPLPROC<=IPLPROC=>EXAMPLE OF USE          |
               |                                           |
               | Step 2     Press the MODE SEL key on the CPU |
               | 4381       Master  Console.  This  is  the  |
               |            fourth key down on the  far left |
               |            row  of  keys.  The  screen will |
               |            clear  and  you  will   see  the |
               |            General  Selection panel, one of |
               |            the CPU Service Panels. Refer to |
               |            Using  the  CPU  Service  Panels |
               |            above    for    instructions  on |
               |            entering   commands    on  these |
               | Level: 2                   Line: 196 of 656 |
               +-------------------------------------------+
```

Figure 10-3.   A screen example demonstrating tiling

Overlapping Windows

Overlapping windows are generally more dynamic with windows placed anywhere on the screen. The windows can overlap each other partially or completely. Usually, the newly opened window is placed so that the previously opened window is still visible and readable to preserve context. This may not be the case if the only context necessary is where the new window came from. In this case only the title line of the previous window may be left visible. This is particularly true when you are using menus in windows to select hierarchical options.

For text displays, particularly those in HyperText systems, it is very important that overlapping windows be positioned so that as much path and context information as possible be preserved.

Overlapping window systems typically allow the user to select as many windows as desired (constrained by virtual storage amounts, perhaps) but even with these systems, limiting the number of visible windows to the 5–7 range is important. This can be done by carefully placing windows if such placement is controlled by the screen driver program. If the user elects to open more than 7 windows, try to restructure the screen so that the 7 latest windows opened are the most visible and obvious. Providing a path for the eye to follow from oldest window to latest one is also helpful. However, older windows may still be high in significance, particularly in HyperText systems where several links may have been activated from the node present in one window. These new windows are more or less equal in significance, and each is only one step removed from the original node. Window placement needs to reflect this appropriately.

Displaying Text on the Screen

The *aspect ratio* of a terminal display is the ratio of screen width to height. Most terminals have an aspect ratio of 4:3. This means that most terminals present text in a landscape mode with the line length being longer than the depth of text on the screen. However, most books use portrait orientation where the depth of the page is greater than the width. There is good reason for this.

The human eye scans left and right in very small increments when reading. If the deflection angle becomes too great several things happen:

- Reading becomes physically tiring.

- The eye loses sight of the left side of the page. This causes tracking errors when a return to the next line is made. The left edge of a page should never leave the peripheral vision of the reader.

- Losing place and tiredness increase the frustration level with the material being read. Consequently, retention and understanding are severely reduced.

When designing any text perusal system, keep in mind the line lengths you are presenting to your readers. While data entry screens can be effective with fields scattered over the entire screen width, text becomes difficult to read when it is spread across too

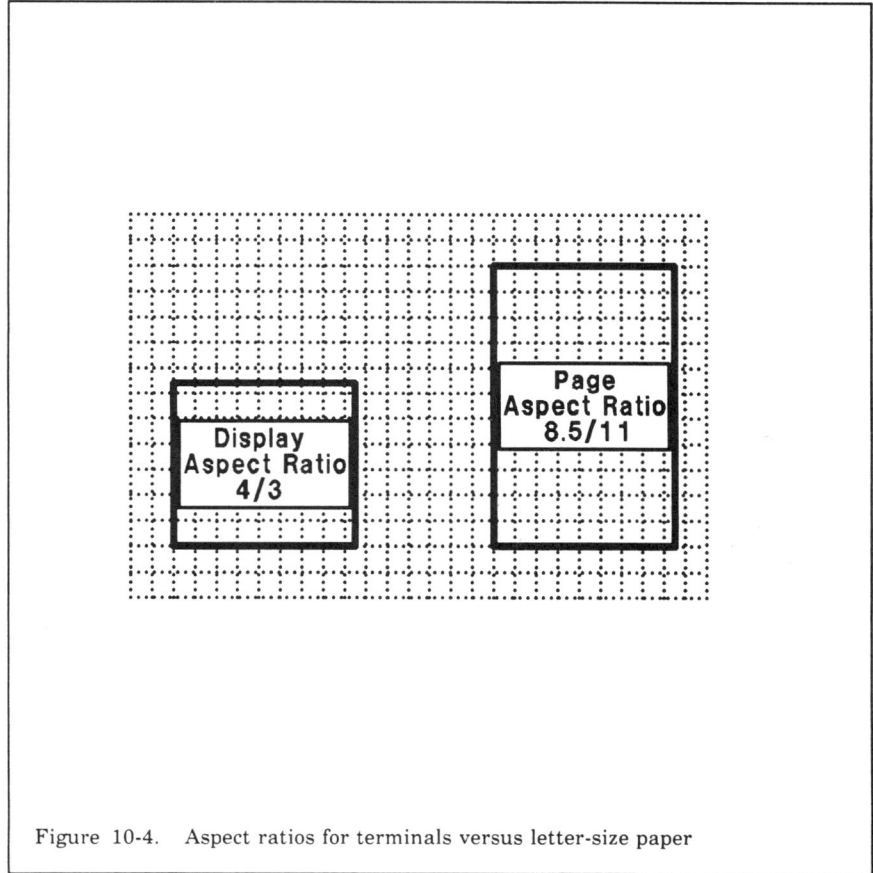

Figure 10-4. Aspect ratios for terminals versus letter-size paper

wide an area. Presenting text in smaller lines within a portrait-oriented column may be a very important step in gaining acceptance with the system you design. This does not necessarily mean that a window interface is required for your system, however. Panels may be constructed around a 60-column line width with a 20-column sidebar for menus and other information. Sometimes, simply composing the text for a 60-column line and displaying it in the center of the screen is the best approach to making the text readable.

On the other hand, a windowed interface may make portrait orientation of the text easier to accomplish. Windows can be sized to present the text in portrait orientation while not having to sacrifice a lot of screen real estate to sidebars or blank space.

Reading Screen Text

This may seem like a strange question, but what *method* do you use to view text? You simply view it, obviously. But it is not that simple.

It is important to design the viewing model for your users carefully, with an eye toward ease of use. For instance, avoid side-to-side scrolling. While people tend to react to up or down scrolling on a screen as a page change in a book, side to side scrolling breaks concentration and makes reading difficult. If your text is too long to fit in a given screen or window width, re-compose the text.

Make it possible to flip pages in the document on the screen. This can be done in several ways:

- Make references to other chapters or sections selectable with:
    ◦ The **ENTER** key
    ◦ The cursor select button
    ◦ A light pen
    ◦ A program function key
    ◦ A touch screen interface
    ◦ A voice interface

- Provide a command line

- Provide an input field just for a new page number

- Provide a rapid viewing mode where each page is displayed in sequence for a very short time until a specific key is pressed

If a HyperText system is being designed, make sure that navigating the network of document nodes is natural, obvious, and easy. Make certain the presentation of the text nodes is done in such a way as to visually provide clues to the relationships between them. This may be as simple as having multiple nodes at a given level not overlap each other, while they do overlap nodes at higher levels.

The methodology you develop for your users to view text is very important and should be chosen with great care. The system should be designed to encourage or mandate the use of a model, and the model should be selected to provide the best interaction and utility to the readers.

Interactive Text Perusal

The text access systems under discussion are all *interactive* in the classic sense applied to computer systems: they are terminal driven and the system performs actions in immediate response to stimuli provided by the user (pressing **ENTER** or **PF** keys, for instance). In this section we want to discuss the concept of interactive or non-passive text access and perusal, where the interaction is between a reader of the accessed text and:

- Other readers of the same text

- The text itself

Interactions with Others

A reader interacts with other readers of a text by making editorial comments. These comments may be verbal (a round table discussion) or written (notes and memos circulated among the reading population). Such interaction may occur synchronously (formal meetings) or asynchronously (memo exchanges and casual conversation).

As you design your text access system, and in consideration of how much time is actually spent interacting with other readers, you should automate that interaction. This facility begins to slip over the line between text-based information systems and what are now known as *cooperative computing facilities* or *groupware*. True cooperative computing systems are well beyond the scope of this book, but an electronic mail or note facility tied into your text access system is not.

Real-time, synchronous conversation about a text object may not be feasible, or truly desirable, for your system. However, asynchronous reader interaction, in the form of notes or electronic mail, *should* be available as a part of the text access system. It should allow a reader to create and send notes to any or all of the people involved in the consideration of a document. Further, it should allow those notes to be created and sent while the reader is still within the document.

It should also be possible to attach the note to a specific portion of the document. If a note is sent while the reader is reviewing something in Chapter 2, it should be possible for the receiver of the note to be positioned at Chapter 2 in the document *by selecting that note for viewing*. This facility is very similar to *annotation*, discussed below. It differs in that it facilitates the interaction of two readers as well as the interaction between a reader and the document.

Interacting with the Text

By interacting with the text itself, we mean **annotations**, as shown in Figure 10-5 on page 145. The ability to add comments and notes about a piece of text in the *electronic margins* is vital to the learning and retention process. It should be considered a priority issue during design.

Annotations should not, however, obscure or distract from the text. A common implementation scheme is to allow the user to toggle between a view of the text that shows where annotations have been made and a view in which the annotation identifiers are not shown. When the identifiers are shown, the user should have the ability to directly access the annotations.

Annotations are often added by opening a window or panel on the screen, entering the desired text, then filing the note in a personal file. Annotations always contain a pointer back to the specific piece of text under consideration when the annotation was made. This allows the reader to view text or annotation, connecting the appropriate comment with the text it was commenting.

Some consideration should be given to making annotations public, private, or both. Public annotations might be cataloged in a *general access file*, which allows the annotations to be shared. A shared annotation could alert a reader to additional information available from another source, or correct a misrepresentation in the existing text until a correction becomes available.

A more common use of annotations is the private note or reminder. These annotations are usually short, cryptic, and of use only to the reader. A *personal access only file* would hold all of the notes a user might write in the margins of a printed copy of a document to help you to understand a concept or related procedure. While you might be limited to a small amount of space on the printed copy, lack of space is not necessarily a problem with on-line

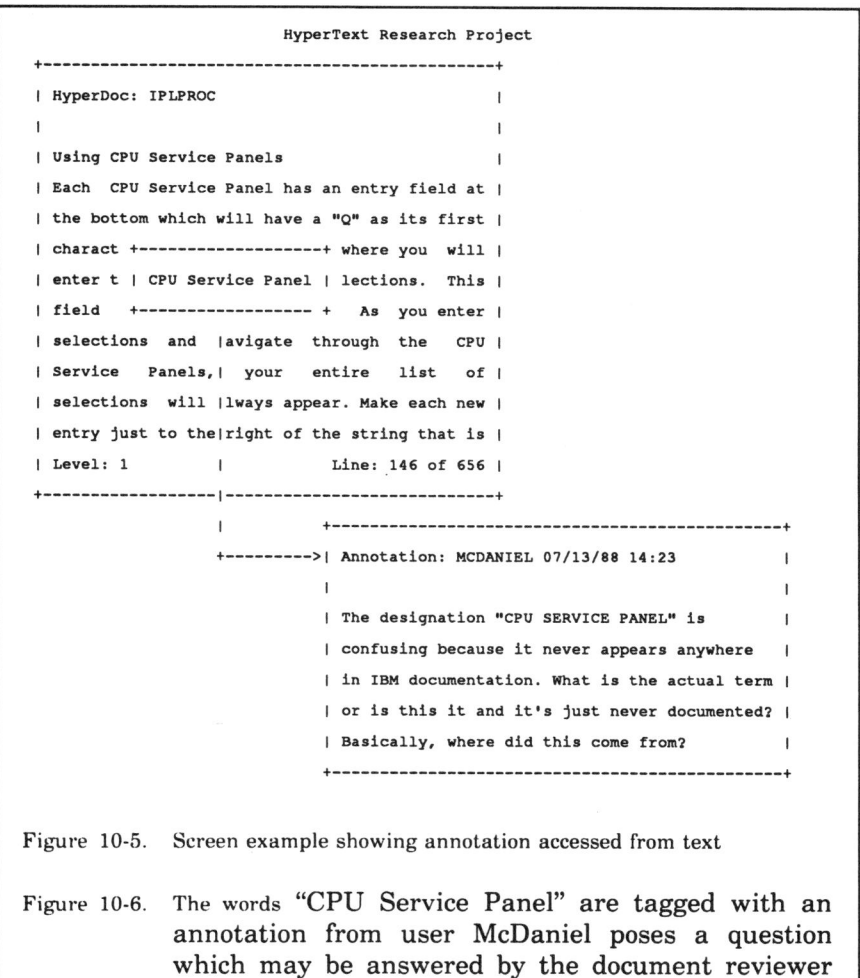

Figure 10-5. Screen example showing annotation accessed from text

Figure 10-6. The words "CPU Service Panel" are tagged with an annotation from user McDaniel poses a question which may be answered by the document reviewer or passed to the original vendor.

text systems. Depending on the design, the annotation facility can allow unlimited commentary.

In systems that have free-flowing annotation ability, particularly where the annotations are shared among readers, it is not unusual to find annotations on a particular sentence or phrase that are longer than the chapter in which they occur. This suggests two additional areas to consider: updating the document and the amount of space permitted for annotations.

How do you maintain consistency between annotations and text when the text is updated? The simplest way is to enforce a two-fold rule:

- An annotation is attached to the nearest heading or subheading in the text, which allows the annotation's pointer to be re-established whenever the attachment moves

- If the heading or subheading changes, the annotation is removed or must be kept attached through a user-driven process.

This technique works on the theory that the annotation is a temporary device for commenting on text that needs revision. If the anchoring text is changed, it is probably because the annotation is being acted upon, thus removing the need for the annotation.

In situations where readers have made personal annotations and the text is subsequently revised, the problem is much more complicated. Before the revised text can be fully integrated into the reader's environment, existing annotations must be re-anchored. If the revisions are not too extreme, this can often be accomplished automatically in the manner described above—anchoring the annotations to headings and subheadings. Any remaining annotations will probably have to be manually anchored by the reader subsequent to the text revision.

Generally speaking, there should be few limitations on the amount of space allowed for annotations. It is probably not necessary to allow more than a single screen for any single annotation, however, as these are intended to be short commentary on either the writing or the subject matter. There should be no limitations on the number of annotations an individual user may make at any point in the text.

Allowing shared-access annotations draws a very fine line between interacting with the text and interacting with the readers. It may be that a shared annotation facility provides enough of an editorial comment facility for your needs.

Ultimate Interactivity

It is not a large step, conceptually, from offering the levels of interaction described above to that of a HyperMedia system that allows users to re-define the flow and organization of their text. This level of interaction is one of the major separation points between HyperText and HyperMedia systems as we have defined them for the purposes of our discussions.

Interaction with the text in such a way that the meaning and context of the text are actually altered are levels of freedom that may or may not be desirable in your system. Before implementing such a system, be sure that your design allows for maintaining the overall integrity of each document within the system.

Allowing a reader to re-organize the information to optimize learning and retention is a desirable goal. Allowing the same reader to misunderstand an important document because of such re-organization is a grave error.

Part 4

Text Member Source Design

It would be ideal to say that there are no special considerations for the creation and maintenance of your source libraries, but this is not the case. Since so many source libraries evolve over time, or are ported into the host environment from environments which permit less user control over the source files, it will be necessary to spend some time looking carefully at the source files as they exist in your environment now and how you want them to be configured when your on-line text display system is completely implemented.

The following chapters provide the guidelines for evaluating your existing environment and for forming the new environment in which your text libraries can perform in both on-line and hard copy environments.

Chapter

11

Evaluating Your Text Library

Your existing text libraries may exist in any of a number of formats and on any number of storage media. Much of the discussion surrounding the evaluation of your existing text library concerns how you currently store your text and how you want to store it when you move into your new environment.

Designing how you store your text members can be as important as the design of the screen layout for using those text members. How you store the members controls how you manage and manipulate them. If you have an existing on-line text library, you have different considerations than those who must create new on-line text members for use with the system. The considerations are slightly different again when you already have an extensive text library, but it exists in a machine-readable format (probably on a floppy disk) for a PC or typesetting system or in typewritten form.

First, let us look at where your library currently exists and review some alternatives for making that library available to your host system.

Existing Libraries

Your existing text library might reside in any number of forms:

- Typewritten
- On a floppy disk in-house
- On a floppy disk at a vendor site
- On your host

This is where we start. Our goal is to have all of the text residing on your host system in files of a manageable size and in such a way that text common to more than one document can be stored in one file which is called by the main document file at composition time. We also want to ensure that formatting-control information is stored separately from the text so that we can use the same text for both hard copy and screen display as easily as possible. If the formatting information resides outside of the document it is possible to call one set of formatting controls when you compose for paper and another set when you compose for the screen, even if this is done as one composition job from the end-user's point of view.

Another goal is to ensure that any time common text is changed, all documents using that source are recomposed to ensure that the most up-to-date versions reside on-line. This poses several problems unless you purchase or develop software that tracks the text members and informs you when a member common to a variety of documents has been changed and what other documents use this information. A variety of text management systems provide this type of tracking, but it would be up to you to integrate it into your on-line system.

A better solution may be to create your composition environment so that each time a member is opened and updated, the filing process causes a check of which documents that file is used within and causes automatic re-composition for all of the documents for both screen and printed output environments. In environments where CPU resources are a problem, you might structure the environment to place all of the composition jobs in a queue for night execution.

From Typewritten Masters

If any part of your proposed on-line text system currently resides in typewritten form only, you have a large task ahead. As described in *Capturing Text* on page 116, you have several choices on how to get that information into your on-line environment. Your options range from scanning to re-keying. You must make the best choice based on the speed with which you need to implement your system and the cost of each option to your organization.

Your remaining considerations are similar to those for people who are creating new text libraries, since you are effectively doing just that. You can control, from the onset, the way text is entered, how text files are named, and how the various text chunks are called together to form a document.

From Floppy Disk

If you have a large library of text on floppy disk or residing on a stand-alone workstation, either in-house or at a vendor site, you must determine how to get that text onto your host system. The difficulty of this process depends on the type of system you currently have in place.

For example, if you are using any of the large number of systems that use the **RFTDCA** (Revisable Form Text Document Content Architecture) format for storing text, you may have an easy way to move these files to your host system.

The IBM Document Composition Facility (DCF) Release 3.2 has an extra cost option called the *Office Document Feature* (ODF), which can be used to import RFTDCA format files to the host so that they can be composed by the DCF program. When the files are ported through this system, the host files may contain a subset of the *Generalized Markup Language* (GML) tags used by DCF or an alternate set of tags called RFTGML; either can be interpreted by DCF during composition. The interpretation can attempt to maintain the formatting that was used in the word processing environment or make changes that present the document in a format using proportional fonts and a more stylish page make-up. After the files are transformed into SCRIPT files, you could choose to maintain the formatting that is there or to modify it based on the full range of options available within DCF.

ODF was designed to import files from IBM DisplayWrite/370 or DisplayWrite TextPak 4 word processing products into the DCF host composition environment. It can, however, also be used to import most RFTDCA documents into the host composition environment.

There are also a variety of other IBM products that may be useful for porting documents from workstation or PC environments, such as the Interleaf Publisher translation facility that ports Interleaf documents to the host system in a format compatible with DCF.

Even without the facilities available in ODF, there are a variety of services that bring data from floppy disk to tape for loading to a host system. Once you have the files on your host, it should not be too difficult to retrofit the formatting controls to the files. You may be able to do much of it by writing a program that interprets the existing formatting and turns it into some form of generalized markup that can be interpreted by your composition system. Alternatively, you could strip all of the existing formatting controls from the files (programmatically or manually) and enter new formatting into the clean files.

How you get your text and formatting control files on the host is not as important as the requirement that you do so.

On Your Host

Another possibility is that you already store your files on the host. Host-stored files may exist as pure text files without any formatting information or as the source for a composition language.

Pure Text Some companies store text in large databases that maintain the text in files segregated by paragraph or topic. These files contain no more formatting than can be done by adding a space at the beginning of a paragraph or a blank line between paragraphs.

One common example is a company that has determined that it is desirable to have the same text used for both the help within an application program and the documentation that accompanies the program. This company could incorporate text that is formatted in this minimal fashion into modules that are called in as part of the executable code in the program.

This text provides a place to start. However, there is no guarantee that the text you deal with accurately reflects the program it describes. Remember that when you begin with existing text, you must still validate the information and proofread the information to ensure that it reflects the program or procedure it is meant to describe.

In the case of the company that has stored the information within the program code, the first job is to segregate those files from the program code and bring them into an environment where composition language coding can be added to them and they can be tested within the new on-line system without touching the actual program code.

Source for a Composition Language You may already have an extensive investment in a text library that resides on your host and contains formatting controls from any of a number of host-based text composition systems, such as the IBM Document Composition Facility (DCF), the Xerox Integrated Composition System (XICS), or the ADR Extended Text Composition (ETC) facility in ROSCOE.

Alternatively, you may be using one of the host-based WYSIWYG document editors, such as DisplayWrite/370. You have the text on the host, but it may not be in a format that you can easily manipulate. If you use DisplayWrite/370, or a product like it that produces RFTDCA, look at the discussion under *From Floppy Disk* on page 153, since that information applies to your environment as well.

If you are already in a host-composition environment, you are one step ahead of the game. You do not need to worry about how to get your files onto the host. You already have the means at hand.

New Text Members

If you know that the implementation of a new on-line system requires the creation of a large number of new text members, either because you have no way of capturing the existing documents in a machine-readable format, or because you are beginning with a new library, you have a few additional considerations.

You must determine the best possible method for moving your information to the host environment. You have two basic options:

- Keying

- Scanning

Each of these options is covered in depth in *Capturing Text* on page 116, but for our purposes in evaluating the text you must understand when each is most appropriate.

Keying

For some documents it is simply not possible to scan the text and produce a file that requires only cursory proofreading and the addition of formatting markup. Text that contains a significant number of equations, graphics intermixed with text, a large number of rules or boxes, and prints in multiple colors requires re-keying. The effort to clean up scanned text would be greater than the effort to simply retype the document.

Scanning

Scanning a document to be marked up with formatting controls requires the use of an OCR (Optical Character Recognition) scanner. Remember that there are two different types of scanners: those that scan the image of the page and those that scan the characters and lines on the page.

You need the latter so that you can manipulate the characters. Even among the various OCR scanners, you must be sure that the one you select, or the one used by your vendor, is capable of handling your text. Some OCR scanners can function only when the text is a fixed pitch font, like those found when the output was created on a typewriter or word processor. More sophisticated scanners can handle proportional fonts, but may not be able to handle multiple fonts on a page or within a text line.

Scanners work best when your text is fairly straightforward. For example, a document that is principally text usually scans accurately, but documents that intermix rules, shading, and graphics with text may not produce a file accurate enough to be of any use.

Text in other than black type may not be read at all. If it is read by the scanner, it is usually quite inaccurate.

As you evaluate your text library you must determine which documents would be scanned accurately enough to warrant using that technology to build your on-line text database and which would be more economically re-keyed.

Remember that even if you choose to scan the document it must be carefully proofread to ensure that letters were interpreted correctly. Scanning does not ensure accuracy, only speed in getting the original text into a file.

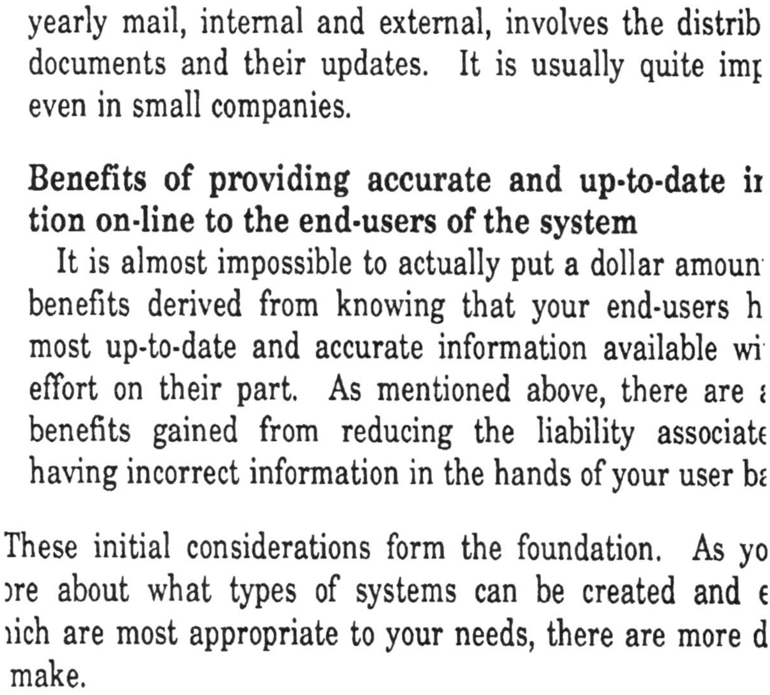

yearly mail, internal and external, involves the distrib
documents and their updates. It is usually quite imp
even in small companies.

**Benefits of providing accurate and up-to-date in
tion on-line to the end-users of the system**

It is almost impossible to actually put a dollar amoun
benefits derived from knowing that your end-users h
most up-to-date and accurate information available wi
effort on their part. As mentioned above, there are a
benefits gained from reducing the liability associate
having incorrect information in the hands of your user ba

These initial considerations form the foundation. As yo
ore about what types of systems can be created and e
ich are most appropriate to your needs, there are more d
make.

Figure 11-1. Scanned image of a text page: The original text was scanned at 300 dots per inch and turned into a bitmap. This type of scanned image can be printed, but it must be treated like a graphic. The text cannot be edited.

Scanning Artwork If your text includes any type of artwork, such as tables, graphics, or photographs, you have some additional considerations based on your intent to display them in your on-line system and how you intend to produce them in paper form. Tables may scan accurately, but not be in a format that is conducive to including markup to reproduce the table accurately.

Any type of graphic poses a similar problem. You may be able to scan the graphic and use its image in such a way that it can be compatible with your screen environment and your paper environment, but this would require the use of graphics terminals for anyone who needed to display the graphic. Often these images, or bitmaps, can be included into the composition system in such a way that they can be compatible with both environments. At this level, though, you simply need to consider your options and your requirements.

Photographs pose much the same problem. Halftone photographs are traditionally created and stripped into a document during the paste-up process. In the electronic environment we need to scan the photograph in such a way that we produce a halftone image, and then use the same process to create a usable graphic object that we would use for any other type of graphic. Many scanners include software to produce halftones in varying resolutions, but remember that you are limited to the resolution of the screen device for display and to the resolution of the printer for hard copy production. This is a restriction you did not have if you produced your documents using traditional printing methods.

Just a Few More Questions

In addition to how and where the text resides, and how to get it to the host, other considerations about your library include:

1. What is the easiest part of the library to make available on-line?

    - Books that are less frequently revised are easier to migrate
    - Shorter documents are better than long documents for the introduction of the on-line documents
    - Books used by a large number of people are good candidates since the users become used to looking for information on-line and are more prepared as the rest of the library becomes available

2. How large is the library?
    The larger the library, the more important it will be to segment the task of migrating to an on-line environment. For a small library (under 50 documents or 5000 total pages), consider migrating the entire library at one time.
    For medium-sized libraries (50–150 documents or less than 15000 total pages), consider creating several separate migration groups by targeting common document formats.

For larger libraries look at the revision cycles of the documents and try to schedule the smallest and least vulnerable for migration first.

3. What is the breakdown on documents that are revised:

    - Never: Do these first. Since they are stable there should be little chance of impacting productivity as you work with the document.
    - On demand, as needed: Begin these after the documents that are never updated and continue to work on them until complete.
    - Annually, quarterly, and monthly: Work these in after the technique is perfected.
    - Daily: Try to do these last to capitalize on refining the migration techniques.

4. Is the text created by one group of people, such as a documentation or publications group? Or, does the text originate in a variety of groups?

    The more centralized your current document creation environment is, the easier it will be to incorporate an on-line methodology to your document distribution. If you have a de-centralized document creation environment, target one group at a time to learn the new techniques, evaluate their libraries, and move into production.

Chapter

12

Configuring Your Text Source

We have talked about how to evaluate your environment to determine your needs, how to decide on the best screen format for your environment, and, in this part, how to review the text that you may already have available to you. Now we want to review some methods for configuring your text source files for ease in management and maintenance.

By *configuring* source files we mean:

- Where should formatting information reside?

- What size should an average text file be?

- How should text files be constructed so that they can be used in more than one document?

- What is the best way to handle updating files used in more than one document?

- How do independent text files gets joined together to form documents?

- What are some approaches to source file management?

Configuring the source file may not be an issue you have addressed. Often the library of source files is built over time by a variety of people, each having their own idea of how to name files to make them easier to find and how to manage the construction of documents. This is the time to re-evaluate your existing methods.

161

Formatting Control—Where Should It Be?

If you have never formatted your files with a composition system that uses a markup language and an independent formatting program, you have probably not addressed the issue of where formatting information resides.

For example, if you have always created text on a typewriter, the formatting information was inherent in the way your typed the document. The same holds true for most word processing systems. What you type and the commands you enter while you type create a document that has formatting controls embedded within it, but which are not modifiable directly by the person entering the text.

If you created host-based documents, but did not use a composition system to control formatting and font selection, you may have created files that were formatted manually by placing extra blank lines in the file, using space characters to indent paragraphs, and underlines or other characters to highlight headings. Or, you may have used a product which did not permit user control of formatting or fonts. Many composition systems do not permit font changes or page layout changes.

In any of these methods, the formatting and the text are not separate entities. If, as you move all of your text to the host environment, you choose to maintain manual formatting, you have no further concerns about where the formatting resides. We recommend, however, that you give serious consideration to integrating a composition system into your environment. With the facilities available in even the most basic composition system, you can create documents that can be formatted for both the screen and printed environments and that take advantage of each environment.

Profiles and Style Files

When you use a composition system to format your documents, you normally have access to services that control the page length, page depth, line length, page margins, and other aspects of the page layout. In most host-based composition systems that are markup-language-oriented, you have the ability to set up files that contain all of the formatting information and maintain those files independently of the text source files. Depending on your environment, this file may be called a *profile*, *style file*, *style specification*, or a *template.* Regardless of the name, the intent is to provide overall document formatting information to the composition program.

If you have a host-based composition system, but have been including all of the page layout information within the individual text source files, this is the time to move to a more streamlined approach. Create a file that defines all of your page layout specifications and any other global information, such as:

- font definitions

- spacing around headings

- page number style

- running heading and footing information and format

- styles for ordered lists

- hyphenation algorithms

Since you are moving into a new era that includes formatting requirements for both on-line display and printed output, you may find that you need a separate file for each of the environments. In fact, if you maintain manuals in a variety of distinct formats, such as marketing material, policy and procedure manuals, user and reference guides, and contracts, consider maintaining separate profiles for each format.

The issue of which profile to select at composition time can be eliminated by the creation of a user interface to the composition system that allows the composer to select the type of manual to be composed, the target environment (on-line or paper), and any other options.

In addition to style files that control global page formatting, you may be using a mark up language that includes a shorthand facility, such as the Generalized Markup Language (GML) provided with IBM's Document Composition Facility (DCF). When such a facility is available, you should consider using it, even to the exclusion of direct formatting markup. One of the features of a GML system is that you mark up a document by identifying the elements to the composition system. In most cases the composition system accesses an additional file to look up the definitions associated to the document elements to determine who is to format them. The type of formatting facility provides the ability to either maintain two libraries of document definitions (analogous to DCF macro libraries), one for the on-line environment and one for the printed environment. Alternatively, you could maintain one library of element definitions that contained internal switches to use slightly different formatting for each environment.

Formatting Differences: On-line vs. Printed

While the goal should be to maintain common source files to produce output for each environment, you may find that the styles you use to present information in a printed format do not lend themselves to the best presentation on-line. For example, list items that are formatted with two line skips between printed items would consume far too much screen real estate if formatted that way for on-line presentation. The amount of space before and after headings is another area where the conservative approach to space will be necessary in the on-line environment.

It would be unnatural to allow the on-line display restrictions to drive how you format the printed text, so the best method of controlling each environment without requiring the text coder or author to be aware of the differences is to confine the formatting information to the style files and markup definition files as much as possible.

How Big Should a Text Member Be?

There are several issues involved in the question of how large or how small to make the source files you will maintain in your overall text access system.

If you are working from files that have been ported from another environment or with files that already reside on your host system, look at how they are configured before you go any farther. Does each document have only one file that contains all of the text and formatting information, or have the documents been constructed so that each part or chapter is in a separate file and is brought together using some type of overall governor file?

With this information in hand, the next question is, how is the on-line system going to access the text? Not technically, but conceptually. Will it access manually formatted text or composed text? We assume that you will use the services of a composition system, which colors our thinking on the subject. However, if you choose to maintain the on-line documents in a manually formatted environment, you may need each paragraph or each displayable entity to be an independent text member.

For most environments, however, the use of a composition system will be the norm. This provides much more flexibility in how the text files are created and maintained, since neither the programmer writing the user interface to view the on-line document, nor the document reader needs to have information about how the source files are configured. This makes it an issue of manageability.

For most environments, documents whose source resides in one giant text file should be broken down into smaller text units. Smaller text units give you the ability to determine if some text units are used in more than one document, and if they are, to maintain them separately from the main files.

One of the goals of developing an on-line information system is to ensure that documents containing common information can be maintained at the same information level with a minimum amount of bureaucracy. If files are organized so that they contain definable subsections and are named so that they are easily associated with what they contain, it is much easier to use information in more than one document. The benefit is that when the information must be updated, only one file must be touched, yet if that file is used in a variety of documents, simply recomposing the documents (if you use a method of text display that uses the services of a composition system) updates them.

In fact, you may want to automate your update cycles so that when a text file is updated, all of the documents which use that file are routed to a batch composition queue, composed, and then placed into the production environment automatically. This function could be further automated to rename the old version and move it out of production.

If you already use a style of document management that calls for the use of smaller files joined together to create the larger main document, review how effectively you are using this technique.

Managing Multi-use Files

To effectively manage files used in more than one document, you should consider creating and enforcing some rigid guidelines for commenting the text, naming the files, and ensuring that updated files are moved in to production for all main documents using the file. Much of this is procedural, although a talented user-interface programmer could automate many of the areas.

First, when each file is created, or carved from a parent document, the file should be commented to show:

- Creation date

- Author

- Primary parent file

- Other main files that will use this text file

- An update history, including reason for the update and source of update information

It may seem that the comments could become larger than the text file. In fact, that can be true. The trade-off is in how much information is available about the text member and its history so that the impact of updating any text member can be assessed quickly by the people managing the maintenance process. If a text file contains only one paragraph, and a small change to that paragraph is requested, it may not seem unreasonable to make the change and move that new file into production. However, if that single file is used in every document in your document library, that single change could mean recomposing your entire document library to make that change available. The impact of such a change needs to be weighed carefully.

Another important point is that text units and their formatting *should* be able to stand alone. They should include not only a complete text unit, but all of the text formatting information required for that text to format correctly in any environment in which it is used. We say *should* because at times it is more desirable to include only text in a text file and exclude formatting information because the formats of the various documents in which the text unit is used are drastically different.

One potential trouble spot is the use of lists. You may encounter situations where not all of the list items apply to all of the environments that use the main list. You might add switches within the source text member to test for the target environment to mask out any unwanted list items, or you might place variable list items into separate files that are only called in when formatting for the appropriate environment. Regardless of the approach you settle on, you must ensure that all of the information required to format the list item correctly is available, regardless of the formatting environment.

Configuring Main Document Files

The same rules noted above for configuring multi-use files apply to the creation and management of what we call *main document files*. This is the term we use to identify an overall governor file that calls in all of the text members needed to create a document and also contains calls to document elements such as the table of contents and index.

Remember that commenting this file is just as important as commenting the text source files. You may want to include comments about what is contained in each file. If some of the files contain nested calls to still other text files, you may want to note that, too. The goal is to provide as much information to someone reading the source for the file as they will require to effectively manage the environment.

Document Management

Every document creator has some type of document management system currently in place. It may be as simple as the names of the documents in the library on a blackboard in the manager's office or something as elaborate as a software-based document version and control system. You must carefully evaluate your current system in light of moving to the more sophisticated on-line text display environment—not because on-line text requires more management than printed text, but because as your environment grows and you want to take advantage of the flexibility available with an on-line display environment, you must know more about the state of all of the documents within the environment. Two ways to track this information are:

- Naming conventions

- Automated document version control

Naming Conventions

The problem of what to call text files confronts every person who sits at a keyboard and uses a text creation product, whether it is PC-based or host-based. The problem is one of naming the file simply, such as *Profile* or *Chapter1*, or to devise an elaborate naming convention, such as *OTDESTXT*.

With the first scenario, it becomes difficult over time to remember which profile the *Profile* text file belongs to. With the second scenario there has to be some known key to decipher the name of the file so you can relate it to a specific document. And what do you do about files used across document boundaries?

There is no correct answer. There are only preferences on the part of every person who manages a text environment. For the most part, however, there is much that can recommend the use of names that target the purpose of the text member.

For example, *OTDESTXT* is the name of the source file for this chapter. The *OT* relates this file to the book *On-line Text*; *DESTXT* relates to the purpose of this chapter, which is the design of text source files. This example does not handle a situation where a file might need to carry its own revision level, or relate to a specific version of a product. It is not a long step, however, to make this type of naming convention work in almost any environment.

In a VM environment you have an eight-character file name and an eight character file type to work with. In an MVS environment you have an eight-character member name which can reside in a data set name that can have up to 44 characters. The data set name is divided into nodes, each of which can be up to eight characters. There can not be more than 22 nodes. File name conventions are illustrated in Figure 12-1 on page 169.

```
VM/CMS File Names:

nnnnnnnn  tttttttt

filename  filetype
```

MVS File Names:

```
aaaaaaaa.bbbbbbbb.cccccccc.dddddddd.eeeeeeee.ffff(mmmmmmmm)
   |        |        |        |        |       |      |
 node1    node2    node3    node4    node5   node6  membername


aaaaa.bbbbb.ccccc.ddddddd.eee.ffff.gggg.hhhhh.iiii(mmmmmmmm)
  |    |     |      |     |    |    |     |    |      |
  n1   n2    n3     n4    n5   n6   n7    n8   n9  membername
```

Figure 12-1.   File naming in VM and MVS

Using a combination of the qualifiers available, you should be able to devise a naming convention for files that will work in any environment.

The added benefit of using naming conventions is that it becomes easier to track how many files comprise a given document. If you adopt a naming convention that also identifies multi-use files with some type of special identifier, it also becomes easier to locate those files.

Automated Version Control

While naming conventions for text files can help in managing the environment, you may already have in place or be considering the implementation of an automated version control system for your document library. Several are available commercially, such as the IBM Publishing SolutionPac ProcessMaster and Image Sciences'

DocuVise. You might also have one that was written in-house or plan to write one. The purpose of automating version control is to gain a tighter rein on the status of each document in your document library and the components of those documents.

If you already have a version control system in place, you should not need to make modifications to it to handle your on-line system, since on-line documents should look to that system just like a paper document. If you are considering purchasing one or creating one, you should make it part of your overall on-line implementation project so that you can ensure that your on-line system and your version control system interface effectively.

Creating Text Members

Our purpose is not to expound on good general writing techniques nor to attempt a comprehensive discussion of technical writing, but to provide some pointers for creating new text files or modifying existing files with the on-line display requirements in mind. There are three main areas of concern:

- General text

- Heavily formatted text

- Including graphics

Remember that there are presentation methods and formatting methods generally used in printed documents that will not work in an on-line environment. Our goal in this chapter is to point out some of the potential problem areas and help you to navigate around them.

General Text

For most documents the text can be created and maintained independent of the on-line or print environment. This is especially true if you use a composition system and a markup language that permit you to redefine formatting for a document based on its environment at composition time. You must still pay some attention to the overall structure of the text files to ensure that you can take advantage of the facilities in the composition system and to ensure that the on-line display system can display them in a user-friendly manner.

First, carefully review your headings and titles. Ensure that they are descriptive on their own and do not rely heavily on surrounding information. In an on-line system the user may be accessing the information from another document or from another area within the same document. The heading must have enough information to provide a frame of reference in which the information is being presented.

Review references to information within the same document. It is not uncommon to refer back to an earlier section or forward to a later section within a document. Ensure that the method you use to make the forward references does not lose its ability to provide information when you move to an on-line environment. For example, a reference that is entered into a document like this:

```
Refer to page 15 in the first chapter for details.
```

loses its effectiveness in an on-line environment. Page 15 in the paper version of the document is probably not panel 15 in the on-line system. Additionally, the reference to the first chapter is ambiguous, especially in an on-line system in which the user may have entered that piece of text through a link from another document.

Instead, the reference needs to point at either a specific section or subsection by name, or to have a reference pointer coded in such a way that the composition system can provide a page number for the printed version and a screen or panel number for the on-line system.

Footnotes and bibliographic entries that are normally found at the bottom of pages in paper documents are not easily displayed in the same format in an on-line system. You have two primary alternatives:

- Design the on-line system to notify the viewer when a footnote or other type of citation is available and provide a function key or command to display the information.

- Rewrite the text to imbed the reference information.

Either will work. Which you select should be based on how heavily you use footnotes and citation material and the types of facilities you want to include in the user interface to the on-line system.

Review your general text environment carefully, and then move on to the more fragile text areas, such as tabular material, columns, and graphics, as described in the following sections.

Heavily Formatted Text

Heavily formatted is the term we use to identify text layout environments that involve placing text in specific areas on the page, either in relation to other text or in relation to margins. For example, tabular information is typically entered on a line-by-line basis and flowed into pre-defined tab stops. If these tabs are defined in qualified space units, such as inches or millimeters, the tabs may not be interpreted correctly or appropriately when formatted for the on-line text environment. If they are defined in terms of the character position on a line, the formatting for the paper version may not be appropriate.

This is one of the situations in which the ability to invoke alternate formatting based on output environment will be necessary if you want to create a solution that requires almost no thought on the part of the text coder or document author, but is sensitive to the different output environments.

If you have a generalized markup language facility you might consider writing a TAB tag to invoke tab processing. Depending on the sophistication of your tab requirements, you may want to have a different tab tag for each of the various tab stops you might require or pass the tab tag parameters for one environment that can be interpreted for the alternate environment by performing some calculations within the tag processing macro.

Another type of formatting that can create formatting opportunities is the use of multiple column formats, especially if the number of columns changes within a document.

The first problem is that multi-column material is almost unreadable on a terminal. Depending on your presentation methods—window-driven or panel-driven—you may find that it is not possible to access the material in a multi-column mode. At this point you must analyze why you have moved to a multi-column presentation in the text, and then determine the most effective presentation for the screen. Again, if you are in a composition system environment that permits the use of a markup language, create an alternate processing environment for the screen that is invoked only when composed for that environment. If the multi-column format was selected to conserve pages, you should not lose any information by moving to single column display on the terminal. If, on the other hand, the columns were necessary to show relationships between entities, you will have to look carefully for the best presentation to the screen. If your multi-column environment involves a definition list in the hanging indent style, you may be able to display to the screen in this format. Alternatively, you might be able to change the material in one column to headings or subheadings and flow paragraphs from the next column under the heading.

If there are areas in your documents where you have used unformatted text, in program listing examples, JCL examples, coding examples, or screen displays, review them carefully to determine if they will overrun the screen boundaries or window boundaries when brought into your on-line environment. You may find that unformatted text presents a larger challenge, since you cannot normally control the size of the type on the screen, nor the number of characters on a line within a JCL example or screen display example.

Where possible, abbreviate or break lines as appropriately as possible. If you do change the appearance of an example to make it fit into the environment, be sure that the on-line version contains a note that it may appear differently in the paper version of the text.

Graphics

Graphics present a special challenge. If you have a terminal capable of supporting the display of graphics, you still may not have the software that permits you to view the graphic on-line. If you have both the terminal and the software, you may still not have the resolution on your terminal that makes viewing graphics worthwhile in your environment.

Evaluate your graphic display needs based on your true requirements. If the graphics are uncomplicated line graphics, they should not present a problem. If you are in an engineering, design, architecture, or other technical environment in which complex graphics are integral to the documents, take the time to investigate all of the display possibilities. You may find that you must maintain complex graphic files for display in a different format than those used for printing, and this extra storage burden may be greater than you want to cope with.

Consider maintaining a line art version of complex graphics for display on the terminal, and a complex version of the artwork for printing, if this is acceptable in your environment. You might also consider displaying a message that notes the existence of a complex graphic that is not available for display but that can be found in the paper version of the manuals.

Part 5

Technical Considerations

In this section we discuss the technical aspects of implementing on-line text access systems in a mainframe environment. We examine several major areas in detail to determine the best text access architecture to use by addressing:

- *Access to text in electronic libraries*
- *Connecting and relating members of an electronic library*
- *Structuring documents in electronic libraries*
- *Document access functions*
- *Processor considerations*

Chapter

13

Access to Text in Electronic Libraries

There are two aspects to the task of accessing text in an electronic library:

- Physical organization of the text as data

- Search and retrieval methods used

Each issue has its own peculiarities. A computer-based system must treat text as data. To do so, the text must be organized into common data structures that can be manipulated programmatically. Then, the access system must lay intelligent text manipulation and management algorithms on top of these data structures. These must make allowances for the vagaries of text. It must be able to access, update, display, and print the text according to the same loose rules that people use all the time with pen, paper, and the printed word.

The algorithms must offer users search and retrieval functions that operate in an intuitive and understandable fashion. People usually look things up in text documents in both an associative and random fashion. On-line text access systems *must* offer these same facilities if they are to be widely accepted and used.

Physical Organization of Text as Data

The treatment of text as data often conflicts with traditional data processing techniques. You must take this into account when designing an on-line text system because the data structures chosen *must* allow for textual variations and ambiguities.

Text is generally free form, with only visual markers for changes and transitions. For instance, paragraph transitions are often recognizable only by:

- The indention of a new line

- A short line ending the previous paragraph

- A blank line between blocks of text

These are difficult to recognize programmatically. Text search algorithms must recognize them, however. It is generally desirable for newly retrieved text nodes to begin display at paragraph or sentence boundaries. To do this, the text must be stored with markers that identify to the driving programs where document elements begin and end. This is not difficult for text stored in an unformatted manner. It is very easy to construct software that can read a free-flowing text marked up in a generalized markup language, such as IBM's DCF/GML, and recognize document element transitions. It is much more difficult to do so with pre-composed text.

Text Access Methods

Computerized access methods typically come in two varieties:

- Non-keyed

- Keyed

Non-keyed access methods merely allow the data to be sequentially passed through a program. The *program* can recognize any desired data and process it specially, but the *access method* is unaware of the special handling.

Keyed access methods allow some form of search *key* or argument to be presented to the access method. Records are only retrieved when they match the key. Typically, intervening records are not accessed at all, particularly by access methods that use some form of direct access technology to skip them. Keys can be as simple as a relative record identifier or line number or as complex as relational database queries that state retrieval criteria using complex Boolean expressions.

In traditional data management systems, keys are well-defined, well-formed entities such as *customer name, account number*, or *zip code*. These are specific fields in very rigidly defined records. The keys are always in exactly the same fields in the records and usually in the same positions in the fields. They are probably unique so that they specifically identify the record they reside in.

Text search algorithms, however, must handle much *fuzzier* keys. Typically, text keys can be anywhere in the records, and allowances must be made for the key information to actually span more than one record. This can be done easily if the entire text can be held in memory, but requires very sophisticated search algorithms for disk based searching. In addition, text keys are generally not unique, leading to problems of ambiguity that must be resolved by using the context the key is found in.

Data Structures

Access methods such as these often expect the data to be in a structured format, with specific information in specific columns or *fields*. Text does not work well with these access methods since text as data is not typically well structured. It is free flowing and random in its patterns. It is a major design challenge to match text data structures with appropriate access methods.

Choosing the data structure for your text is complicated, but not impossible. There are several traditional data structures that do handle text well when combined with advanced access techniques. Among these data structures are:

- **Variable length records**

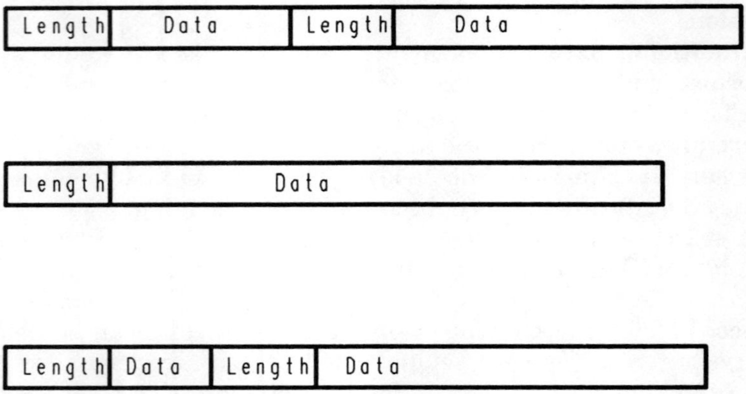

180 On-line Text Management

```
         ┌──────┬──────────┬──────┬──────────────┐
         │Length│   Data   │Length│     Data     │
         └──────┴──────────┴──────┴──────────────┘

         ┌──────┬──────────────────────────────┐
         │Length│           Data               │
         └──────┴──────────────────────────────┘

         ┌──────┬──────┬──────┬──────────────┐
         │Length│ Data │Length│     Data     │
         └──────┴──────┴──────┴──────────────┘
```

Figure 13-1. Variable-length record structure

This structure conserves space when text lines do not all flow to the same length.

- **Partitioned data sets (PDS) or libraries**
  Each chunk of text can be manipulated by name as a *library member*.

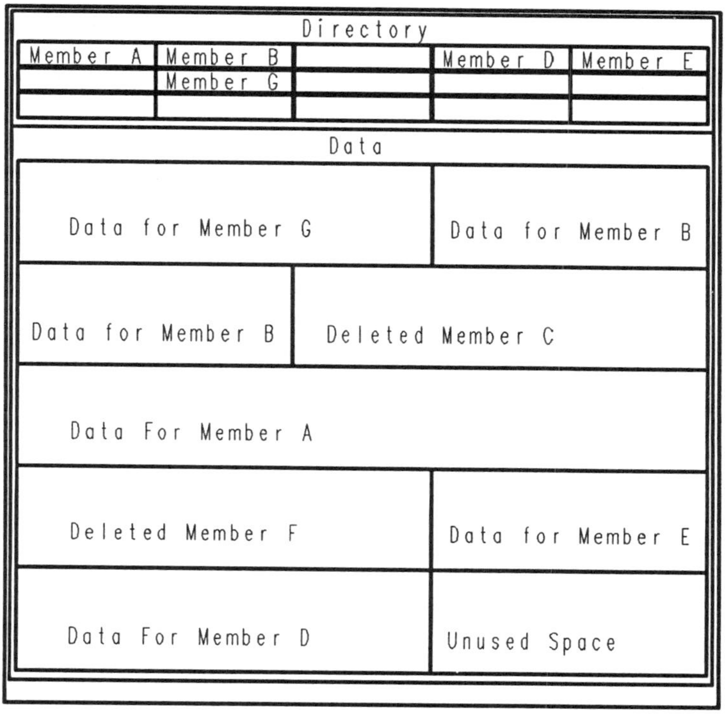

Figure 13-2. Partitioned data set structure

- **Typed records**

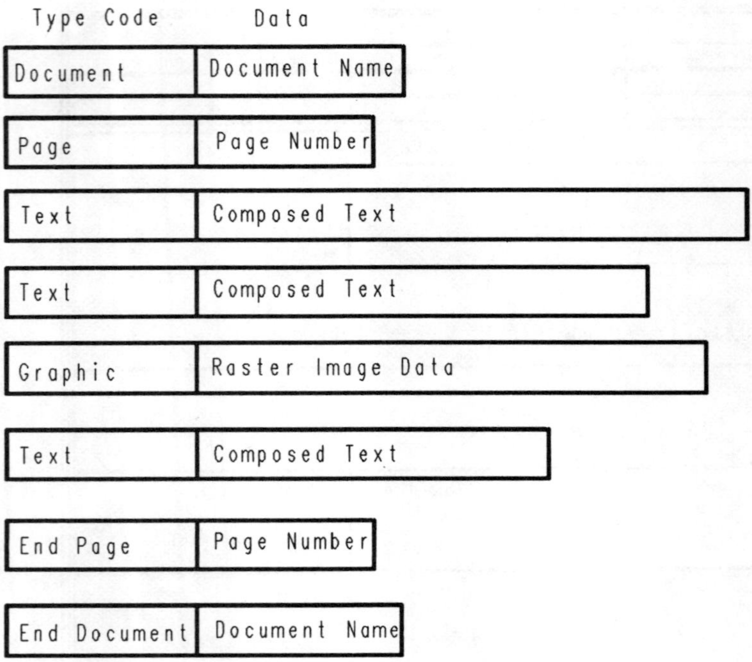

182 On-line Text Management

Type Code	Data
Document	Document Name
Page	Page Number
Text	Composed Text
Text	Composed Text
Graphic	Raster Image Data
Text	Composed Text
End Page	Page Number
End Document	Document Name

Figure 13-3. Typed records

Each physical line of text has a type code added to the front to indicate its document element status. The first line of a new paragraph might have a **P** in the type field, while ordinary text records have a **T** in their type fields.

- **Streamed records**

  Text lines are delimited by characters in the physical records that indicate the beginnings of new lines or spacing on the screen.

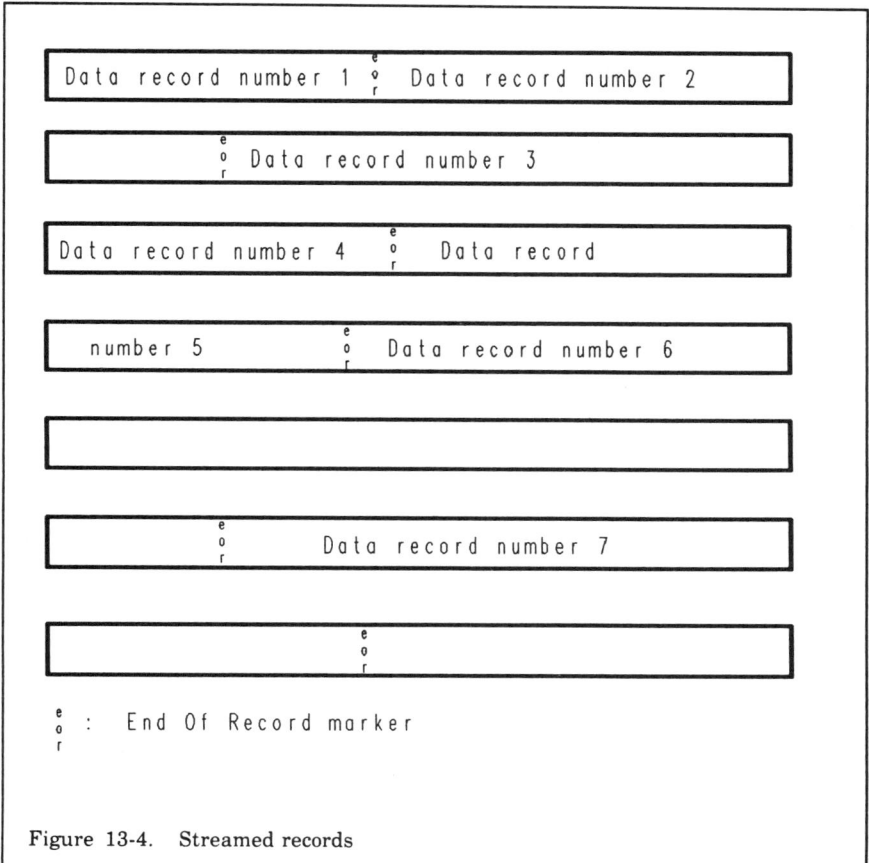

Figure 13-4. Streamed records

Again, these are only a few of the data structures that can be used to represent text. Many of them require some sort of hierarchical definition structures and indexes that reside in other files to impose more formal structure on the text records. There are also inappropriate data structures for text manipulation. Typically, such structures are used when an existing tool, such as a database manager, is used to provide software support for data it was never intended to deal with.

A classic case is the attempt to coerce relational database managers to operate on free-form textual information. It can be made to work; it cannot be made to work well. Database systems offer very sophisticated search and retrieval algorithms for data in their structured file formats. Unfortunately, searching random text records for specific criteria is usually the thing a relational database system does worst. Its free-form compare facility must be used to locate records that contain the search criteria somewhere in one of its fields. The field must have been defined as a line of text and the entire line must be scanned for the desired information. Relational database systems typically do this by brute force. They are designed for structured, well-behaved data that resides in fixed-length fields in the same location in each record; or, at worst, is addressable through length fields appended to each data field. These systems are optimized for their particular purposes, but scanning free-form information is not one of those purposes.

We recommend data structures that remain as close as possible to the original text line format. Encoding document elements into separate records or type fields in each text line is a valid approach, but the important thing is that the actual text remain as close to its original, printable or viewable form as you can manage.

Search and Retrieval Methods

We discussed some search methods above since the problem of data structure choice is tightly bound to the decisions you make regarding search methods. We continue the discussion of search and retrieval methods to show that text is best searched in a heuristic and dynamic manner. Access methods that rely on fixed positions, characters, or hierarchies do not typically function as efficiently against free-form text as they do against structured data. Most do not perform well against even well-structured text if the structure includes variable length fields.

Take IBM's VSAM Keyed Sequential DataSet (KSDS) structure, for instance. A VSAM KSDS must have a specific, contiguous key field defined in the record. Keys that are shorter than the defined key length can be presented, but they must start at the left edge of the field. And keys must be unique. Alternate keys that remove many of these restrictions are allowed, but each alternate index requires its own index dataset, its own contiguous, left-aligned key field, and its own logical I/O path. Neither primary nor alternate keys allow free-form searching, and, if the text is modified, the entire *upgrade set* of alternate indexes must be individually updated. This is simply not viable for massive text databases.

There are access methods and search and retrieval strategies that operate efficiently against text as it is ordinarily stored. These are often called *content-based access methods*. Content-based access methods are designed to index the entire text file, provide free-form searching facilities that are optimized for text, and minimize the amount of I/O activity required to accomplish these tasks. There are several content-based techniques, but they all index the content of the text using the pattern of its information rather than the data it contains, such as IBM's Contextual File Search product.

Here we make a distinction between data and information. **Data**, by this definition, is the collection of binary bits, the bytes, represented in a record. Each byte has nothing to do with its surrounding bytes from a searching point of view. *Information*, on the other hand, is the pattern of bits and bytes representing concepts in a record. An example of data is a record that contains the bytes *X'E3C8C5'* in hexadecimal representation; an example of information is the record that contains the word *THE* in English. Content-based access methods are aware that information is represented by the data. They search and retrieve text based on the informational pattern, not the data content.

Doing this is a subtle process; doing it quickly is difficult. Some access methods produce lists of every word in a piece of text, throw away noise words like *a* and *the*, then maintain pointers to every place other words occur. These are known as inverted list access methods. Others use the numeric values of characters as coefficients to hashing functions, producing mathematical models of the text. Content-based access methods offer a tremendous amount of power and flexibility in text search and retrieval.

It is easy to construct content-based access methods that work, but not easy to make them work quickly. The best techniques for speed involve very complex algorithms that may even be aware of the position of the disk and records on the disk as it spins. There are commercially available versions of these access methods, and you should investigate them while planning your system.

Chapter

14

Connecting and Relating Library Members

In any library system, whether manual or automated, it is necessary to relate one body of text to another and often to many other documents. In manual systems this is handled by bibliographies, concordances, and indexes. In automated systems it is also handled in a variety of ways, many of which are automated versions of the relationships listed above. However, automated systems allow new types of connections and relations between documents to be defined, offering much greater facilities for interdocument search.

Several different techniques for interrelating documents and document elements are available. In particular, since it is the document interrelations that make it unique, we discuss HyperText techniques for interrelating documents in some detail. Beyond HyperText, however, we examine some of the more traditional techniques for interrelating documents.

HyperText Interrelating Techniques

How documents interrelate in HyperText systems is what sets HyperText systems apart from traditional text management and organizational systems. The connections between documents are defined as *links* that carry semantic information.

Links can occur between any two pieces of text. Multiple links can emanate from a single piece of text and a single piece of text can be the target of several links. Any two text *nodes* can be connected by more than one link.

Links typically have names that identify their purpose and provide semantic content for the viewer. The *link type* may indicate how the target node is to be handled with respect to the source node. For instance, some links indicate that a process is to be executed using the source and target nodes as input information. An example might be a link between two spreadsheets that, when activated, calculated a set of statistics comparing one spreadsheet to another.

Many HyperText systems define links as being *directed*. In such systems the links have a direction as well as two endpoints. Therefore a link proceeds in a single direction, from the source node to the target node.

Some systems do not define their HyperDocuments (the overall set of documents connected by links in a HyperText system) with directed links, but do use a network of interrelated links. In a network system a link inherently points both ways. Interrelated information is treated as being on the same semantic and symbolic level; it is not organized in a hierarchy.

Both designs have advantages and disadvantages. HyperDocuments are easier to traverse, but related pieces of information may not be readily available. For instance, in a directed link system it may not be as easy to enter the HyperDocument at any point and still find all the desired information. A structure is imposed on a user's search strategies that may not be natural. Networked, non-hierarchical systems avoid this since all links between nodes are available regardless of the start point, although such systems can be very confusing and difficult to navigate. A potential problem is the tendency to create self-referential loops in networked HyperDocuments.

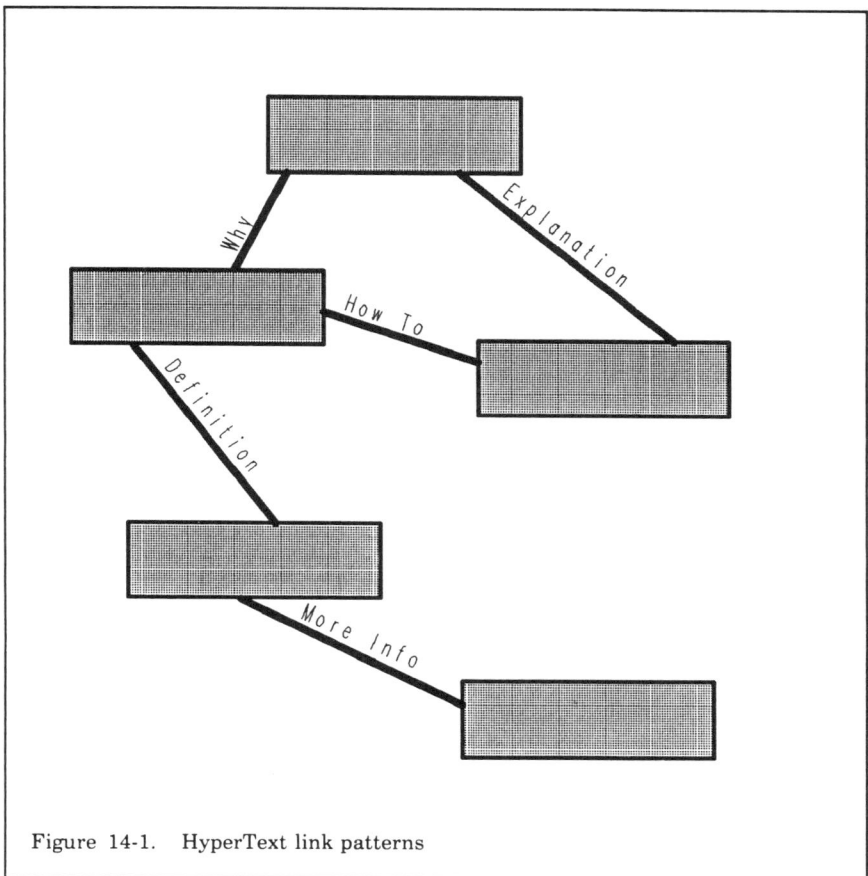

Figure 14-1. HyperText link patterns

The amount of semantic information inherent in the link is also a contributor to the usability of a HyperText system. Some systems only allow predefined link types, others merely place a name on the link with no inherent meaning associated with it. Still other systems form a hybrid between these two extremes, allowing many user-named links while offering some pre-defined ones as well.

In addition to the link name or type and any meaning that may be associated with it, some systems offer the ability to assign programs or processes to links. In this way the selection of a link by a reader activates the process as well as accessing its associated piece of text; indeed, it may only activate the process that may access the actual target node.

Link Management

Developing a HyperText system means developing a huge collection of link information. The structure and topology of the links is not inherently visible to the reader. Consequently, it can be very confusing to traverse HyperDocuments. Readers find themselves lost in a sea of interrelated text nodes, with little or no idea of why they are there. Link management techniques can be implemented that ease the burden to readers considerably.

Whatever design you choose when evaluating HyperText systems, hierarchically directed or networked, be sure that certain link management features are included. What are known as *I ref it* and *it refs me* lists are vital to the management process. These are exactly what they sound like—inverted lists selectable from target text nodes that identify what links emanate from or terminate at the current target node.

Another link management technique you may want to consider a graphic-based document structure *browser*, as illustrated in Figure 14-2 on page 191.

A *browser* is a utility that allows the HyperDocument's internal link structure to be displayed at a glance. On workstation systems this is often a highly graphic display with spidery networks of lines emanating and terminating in boxes with document names on them. The lines are links and the boxes are text nodes. By zooming in on a specific area, the reader can see much of the local structure of document interrelationships. On mainframes such a display is typically not possible or desirable, but a similar *roadmap* can be built by showing an indented list of the document names with the connecting link identified between them.

One word of caution about browsers. Many HyperText readers find them unneeded, particularly if the link names provide sufficient information for intuitive retrieval. Before spending a lot of time and effort developing a browser, make sure your users need one. Authors of HyperDocuments, however, often use the browsers during writing to remain organized and to see that their writing is connected as it should be.

If you are primarily concerned with the ability to peruse a library of HyperDocuments, the browser may not be as critical a feature as much of the HyperText literature will lead you to believe.

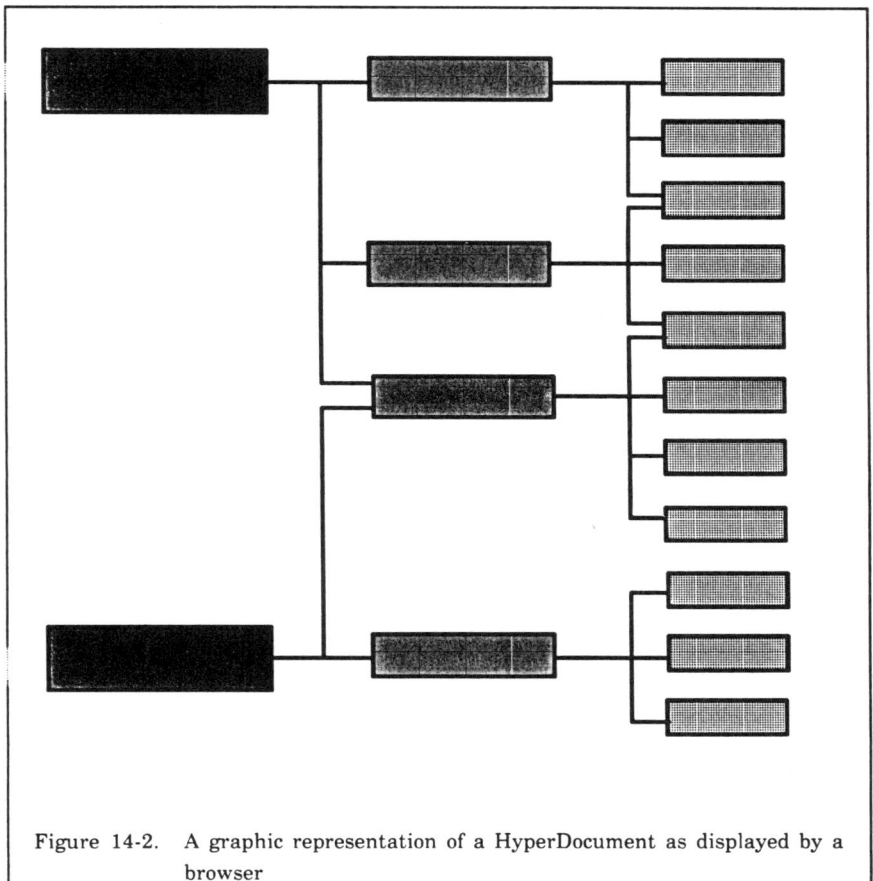

Figure 14-2. A graphic representation of a HyperDocument as displayed by a browser

Other HyperText Facilities

HyperText systems should offer other connection and interrelation facilities aside from links. The text still requires standard indexes and bibliographies if only to provide references outside the HyperDocument. A standard table of contents is also important, even if each item is a HyperText node in its own right. Many systems are organized this way. However, just being able to select a table of contents item from a screen and have the system open that page directly *does not define a HyperText system*. Be sure that other HyperText features are present.

Any HyperText system should also offer, to some degree, the methods of text interrelation we discuss in the next section.

Traditional Interrelating Techniques

Traditional methods of interrelating text elements in any sort of document still have applicability in on-line text access systems of any type. Much of the *connectedness* of a document is implicit rather than explicit. In most documents this connectedness within a document is embodied in the structures such as:

- Heading references
- Citations
- Footnotes
- Bibliographies
- Indexes

All of these types of references must continue to be available in any on-line text access facility, including a HyperText-based one. It must also be possible to easily navigate the system using these references. For instance, there should be a function key to get you to the table of contents, one to get to the index, and, if it is included, one to get to the bibliography.

Citations and footnotes often reference other works that may not be on-line. If they are on-line, you should provide the link to the document if at all possible. If the document is not on-line, offer sufficient information to allow you to locate the referenced publication quickly and easily.

Some documents collect all notes at the back of a book. This may be more appropriate for on-line documents where it can be difficult to separate footnotes from other text using different fonts, as it is typically done on paper. If you elect to use the note appendix strategy, be sure that, at any reference to a note, you can use a function key to jump to the note appendix and enter it at that appropriate citation.

In windowed systems the path taken to the display of a particular window can easily be made visually obvious. Windows can overlap each other providing visual clues to their hierarchy. Panel-driven systems, on the other hand, do not easily offer such clues. In such systems it is important that you indicate why a particular panel is visible. For instance, if you have jumped into the index to search for a reference, there must be some indication such as a header line to tell you where you came from into the index. The system must also allow you to return to your starting point in one keystroke.

At the same time, the index panel should allow you to go directly to a new panel referenced by the index, then return either to the index or to the original panel.

Bookmarking

The above technique is part of a larger technique called *bookmarking*, which is of considerable importance to HyperText systems, but which is very useful in linear systems as well.

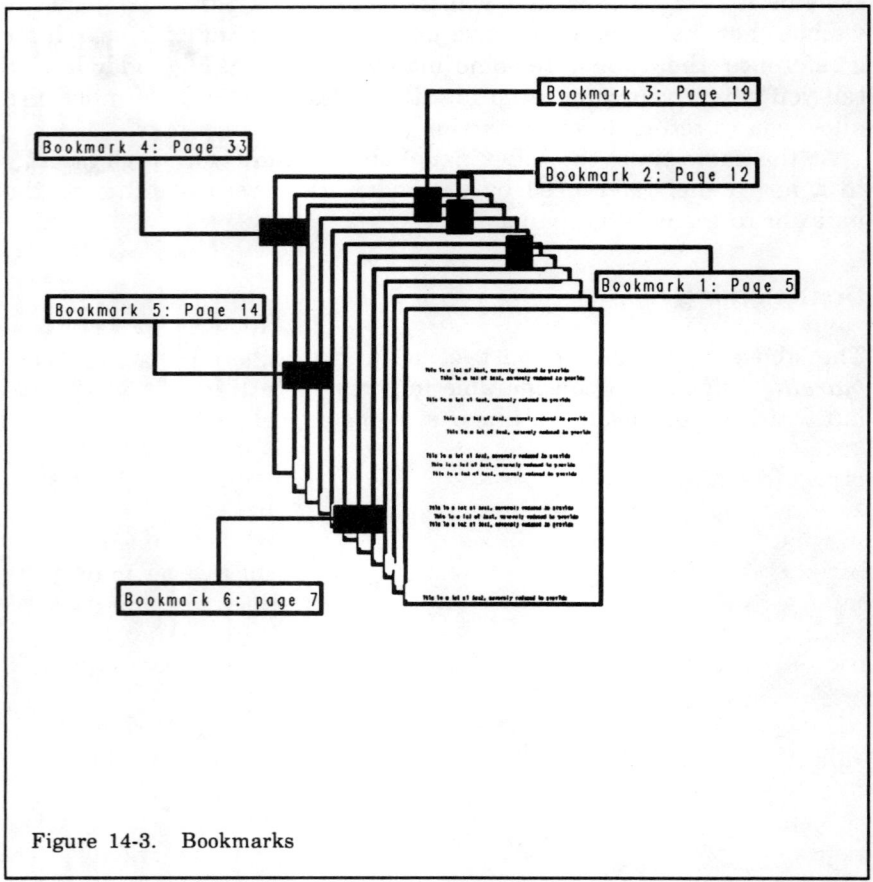

Figure 14-3. Bookmarks

It is useful to be able to "stick a finger into the book" or to "paper clip pages" for quick return. These techniques make it possible for readers to interrelate text in their own fashions.

Look carefully at your user base and the types of documents they use to determine which interrelating techniques should be a part of your on-line system. Do not forget to allow for the re-positioning of heading references, citation references, and bookmarks after an update has been applied to a document. This should be invisible to the person using the document. Remember that the more complex the connections and relationships, the smarter your programming must be about how it cleans up after updates.

Chapter

15

Document Structures Within Electronic Libraries

When designing or evaluating an on-line text access system it is important to consider the structure of the document data files themselves. Relations between documents, such as those discussed in the previous chapter, are typically stored in standard data files and use fairly standard data structures. A relational data base may even prove to be the most useful and appropriate vehicle for this type of information. Document text, however, has a structure that does not always conform to traditional data structures and consequently needs to have special treatment.

Documents can be organized in many ways using different structures. The most appropriate technique to use depends on the document, the scenario of its use and other factors. When choosing an organization for your documents, determine what types of documents you will be dealing with most, then choose an organization appropriate for those documents. It is possible to organize all documents using the optimal approach for each one, but that can pose a host of problems. Start small, using a single organizational technique, and expand it as necessary.

Some of the ways text can be organized within a computer system are as:

- A tree

- A network

- A set of relations or tables

- A simple linear list
- A HyperDocument

Each of these structures has benefits and drawbacks. We discuss each one with examples of an appropriate instance of its use.

Tree-structure Documents

Documents organized into trees follow fairly typical paper document conventions. There are sections, subsections, chapters, subchapters, pages, and paragraphs. The main difference between on-line tree structure and a paper book is in access techniques.

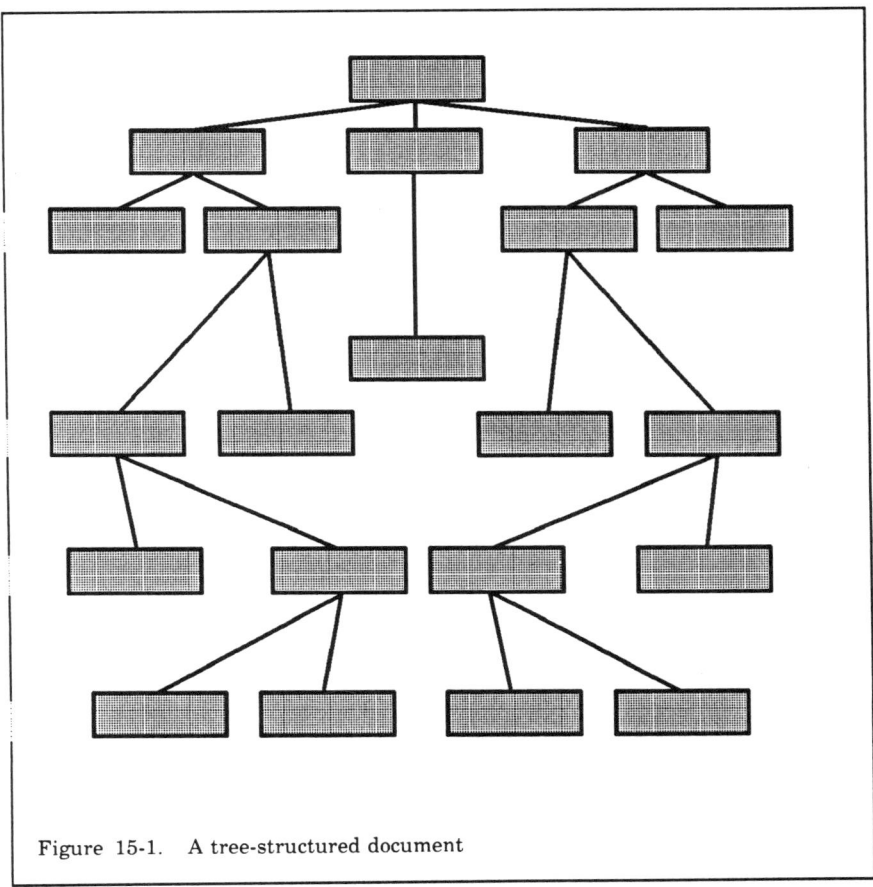

Figure 15-1. A tree-structured document

Tree-structure documents are rigidly defined so that any movement between major branches of the tree requires returning to a branch point higher near the top of the tree, then following a branch outward to a different area. There is no lateral jumping between branches, and readers on one branch are often unaware of other branches.

Tree structures are good for help and menu systems where access to the text needs to be under rigid control. In a help system, there is often a desire to keep the reader focused on the task at hand and not allow wandering into other topics. This is a natural desire since the goal of a help system is to increase productivity rather than impacting it. Forcing a return to a higher node or branch point, such as the screen from which help was requested, allows the designer to exercise control over the user's perusal activity.

Network Document Structures

Documents organized as a network allow more lateral movement without the constraints of tree structures. There is usually some method of simply specifying a page number or a chapter title to the system so that the text can be re-entered at that point. This is akin to a paper book where you can flip to any page or chapter by scanning running headings or footings while riffling pages.

Networked documents lend themselves to tutorials and general reference documents where the author wants the reader to follow associative research techniques. There are usually function keys that return the user to major points in the book, such as table of contents or index, but networked documents also allow for simple, linear page turning.

Relationally Structured Documents

We have stated earlier that relational databases do not lend themselves to text storage and retrieval as well as other strategies. Nonetheless, they may be made to work with a degree of efficiency. They may be used where a decision has been made that relational technology is to be implemented across an organization. They can be best used for single-item retrieval systems like help systems or encyclopedic references. They do not lend themselves to associative search because the database managers do not usually offer powerful enough access methods for searching long strings of text.

Relational systems can be most effectively used to store information about the documents. In this manner, they are able to handle *meta-knowledge* about the document library, while the text is structured in a different manner altogether.

Linear Documents

Often documents are structured and presented in a simple linear manner. This structure lends itself to systems where small pieces of self-contained text are useful, such as previewing systems. The documents are generally stored as a set of sequential files or members of a library. The only indexing available for them is

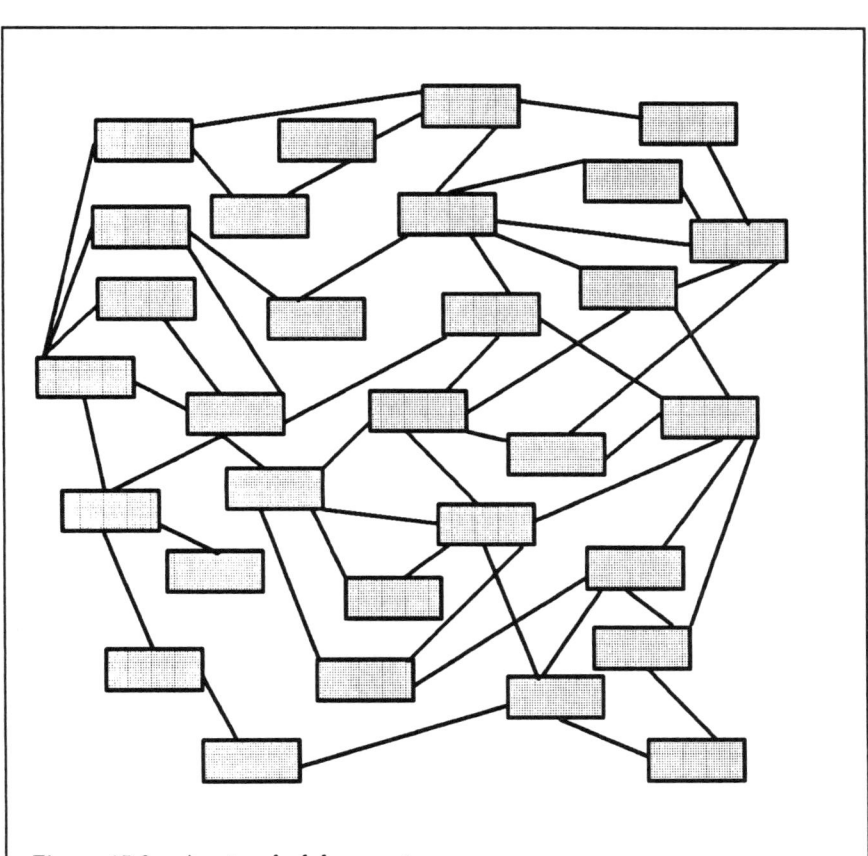

Figure 15-2. A networked document

usually that of the library or disk directory. Once a given document is retrieved, there may be some associative searching capability, but only against the current document. There is generally no ability to search across documents or document elements.

Linear organization is useful where simple presentation is to be done, where little or no searching is expected, and where text can be easily broken into small chunks. However, if there are too many text chunks the user has a problem with maintaining any sense of structure to the system. The only organizational tool is the directory, and the classic problem of trying to devise mnemonic document-naming standards quickly arises. Documents organized in a linear manner can work for a while, but in almost all situations they

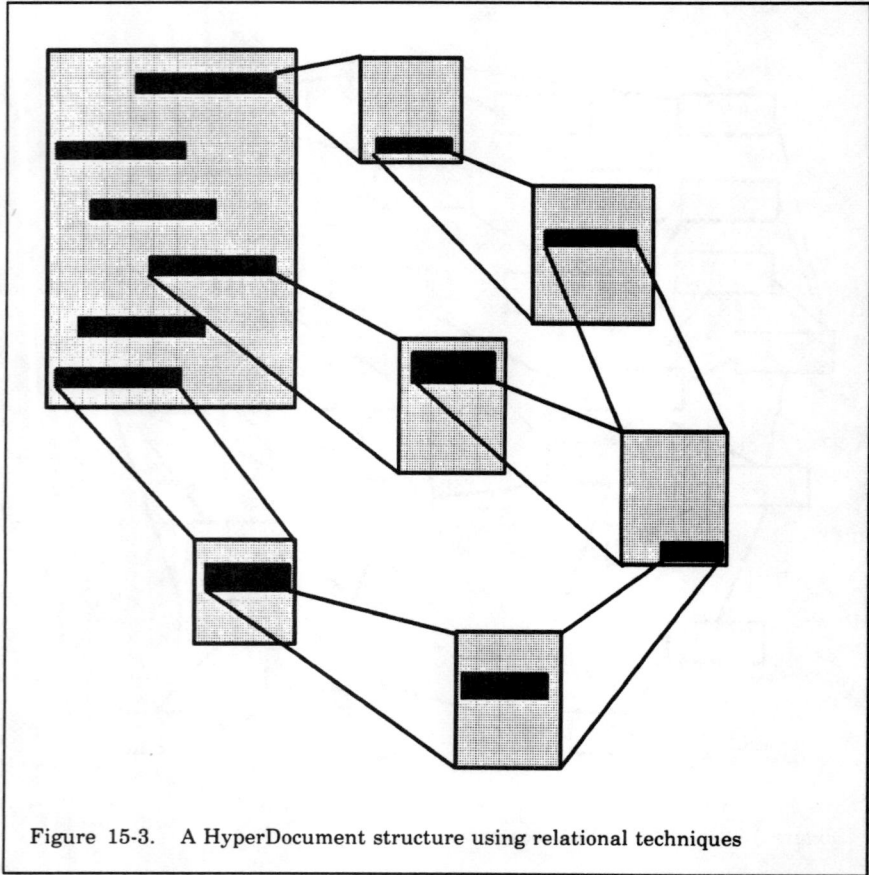

Figure 15-3. A HyperDocument structure using relational techniques

rapidly break down into chaos, and a more sophisticated structure is required.

HyperDocument Organization

HyperDocuments are organized for rapid associative search, but elements are connected with semantic links. These links form a network, but one that is more detailed and more easily navigated than the networked structure described above. The links may reside in a relational database, as they generally have the appearance of tables, but the actual text typically resides in sequential files that can be randomly addressed and searched. Obviously, a HyperDocument makes use of all of these structures.

HyperDocument structures are most useful when large volumes of intricately interconnected text needs to be read in a non-linear fashion. Sophisticated associative search strategies are typically made available that may cross document boundaries. The links themselves form an associative search network if they are given names that help indicate their purpose and meaning.

Systems that benefit from HyperDocument organization are user manuals and other forms of instructional material, highly detailed historical or reference material that depends heavily on other work, and documents designed specifically to aid research into a given set of topics.

Document Access Functions

We have already discussed in some detail several aspects of document access:

- Sequential

- Indexed

- Associative

- Linked

While these topics cover the usage aspects of document access, there are other considerations as well. Documents can be accessed:

- By programs other than the on-line text system

- From near-line as well as on-line sources

- Directly from memory

These all represent techniques for using documents somewhat outside the on-line text system; you do not have to consider these aspects of document access if you stay safely within the confines of your system. During design or evaluation, consider providing the ability to retrieve and access the document from a program other than the base on-line text system. The access should be simple, should return the document in a data structure your program can deal with, and should be available from several different languages: Assembler, high-level compiled, and fourth generation.

It is important to remember that you will not always have sufficient on-line storage (DASD or Optical Disk) to hold all the documents you have available for retrieval. Studies indicate that most documents follow a retrieval curve: 80% of the retrieval against a document is performed during the first 20% of its life within a given system, be it manual or computerized. After that it tapers off quickly. This means that near-line retrieval can be important. You should move documents out of your on-line facility into some slower, but still digital storage medium, probably tape. Be sure that your system provides simple and user-transparent retrieval of these documents. From a user's point of view, the only difference between retrieving an on-line document and a near-line document should be time. The near-line document retrieval should still operate within a time frame that is acceptable to the on-line user. It may take minutes, but it should not take hours.

Another aspect of document access is that of *in memory* documents. It may be possible to pre-load often-used documentation into memory and have it available both to the on-line system and to other programs. If you take this approach, be sure that the data structures used are well supported by your programming languages. Also be certain that your computer system can afford to have the documents resident in memory. This can dramatically improve retrieval times, but can consume a large portion of your system resources. A final consideration for in-memory access is that, as with near-line retrieval, the actual interface to the retrieval process should be transparent to the casual user.

Chapter

16

Processor Considerations

What loads do an on-line text system put on your existing computer system? By the term *load*, we mean the burden placed on your computer system by users accessing the system and interacting with the files stored on the system.

What considerations are there for processor response and power?

These questions are very significant for text perusal systems for a variety of reasons.

The intent of your text access system is to display text on the screen for viewing and reading. You are attempting to replace printed media, at least to the extent of limiting the number of copies you reproduce and distribute. Generally, there is a desire to improve the productivity of your staff by reducing the amount of manual effort required for researching a question. All of these desires are thwarted and the benefit of on-line text lost if the processor running the application is underpowered.

There are many things to consider in evaluating the load placed on your processor by such a system.

- Page transition time

- Search algorithms

- Multi-tasking processes

- Graphics

- WYSIWYG text display

Page Transition Time

When reading a book, turning a page is virtually instantaneous. It actually takes about half a second, on average, but the time is completely ignored by the reader. This *page transition time* is one of the most important variables to optimize in an on-line system. It should be kept under one second.

The time shifting from one screen of text to another is time in which the attention of the user strays and can be lost. Since on-line text presentations typically display much less text than books do on a single *page*, less information is available to hold the reader. This leads to a situation where even a two-second delay can cause the reader to lose context and short-term retention of the material.

If it is not possible to reduce the page transition time to a sub-second response, the delay can be made tolerable by using certain screen design tricks. For instance:

- Keep the screen from flickering or blinking between pages

- Keep the current page readable while waiting for the next

- Offer some motion on the screen to indicate that paging activity is taking place.

Some systems clear the screen and repaint each line of the new page just to give the illusion of activity. Others place a flashing message at the bottom, very inconspicuously, while text search is going on. The motion increases the time sense of the viewer and even a four- or five-second wait seems faster.

Consistent response time is also very important. Offering half-second response time on one page turn and eight-second response on the next leads to an incredible frustration on the part of the user. It is far better to have a consistent four-second page transition time.

Users are also much more willing to wait when they perceive an operation as being time consuming. Turning to the next page of text is considered trivial; searching for a specific string in a 500-page document is not. The amount of time a reader is willing to spend on a reading task depends largely on how the reader perceives the time requirements of the task. Displaying successive page numbers during a search or having the total number of pages left in the document somehow visible to the user can alter the perception in favor of the system.

Search Algorithms

When text is searched, much computer power can be consumed performing inefficient tasks. A prime example of this is the string-matching technique used by most mainframe editors.

1. The search argument is accepted from the user.

2. The first character is extracted.

3. Each record is retrieved and scanned for any occurrence of this character.

4. If a match is found on the first character, the entire search string is compared against a segment of the record starting at that character's location.

5. If a match is not found, the character scan starts at the next character in the record.

6. The process continues, scanning across each record and comparing whenever the first character is found.

This is not a bad algorithm, particularly if the file being searched is already contained in virtual storage, but it can be dramatically affected by the construction of the search string. For example, the accepted sequence of the first six most commonly used letters in English is *ETAOIN*.[2] Therefore searches for strings starting with *E* should take longest, because there are so many to be checked.

For simplicity's sake we assume that the search treats upper- and lowercase letters as being equal and that the search is to scan all records in the document to let you know how many occurrences there are of a string.

Using this reasoning, searches that begin looking for strings beginning with *E* are less efficient then those beginning with *Z*.

But are the differences great enough to make a difference?

In one of the early draft versions of the file containing the text you are reading now, there were 93,456 characters with the following distribution of letters:

---

[2] Computer Recreation, *Scientific American*, October 1988, p. 145

- 4207 Es
- 3173 Ts
- 2485 As
- 2146 Os
- 2353 Is
- 2175 Ns
- 37 Zs

These do not seem to be significant enough to matter to a computerized search algorithm, but we have left a character out of our consideration. What if our search string starts with a *blank*? To the search algorithm we described above, the blank character is a character just like any other. In this file of 93,456 characters, there are 60,135 blanks!

If you constructed a search argument beginning with a *blank*, it would find 14 times as many first-character matches as a search argument beginning with E. This is a very significant difference.

The algorithm could be improved by having it scan records for the first non-blank character of the search string, then back up to compare the string with the blank. It could be further tuned to always scan for the character in the search string least likely to occur, but the programming to accomplish that would probably eat away at the searching efficiency gained.

The point of this discussion is to illustrate that search algorithms are critical; use of a search argument that is inefficient for the algorithm can devastate performance. Typically, the more complex the search, the longer it takes. Many searches allow multiple arguments combined into a Boolean expression. The most advanced algorithms can even perform *fuzzy search*, where records that almost match the argument are retrieved. This gets into the area of artificial intelligence and its applicability to text search.

Your users should not have to be aware of these considerations, and they should not have to construct their search arguments in any constrained manner. As designer or evaluator, you should verify that the algorithms used by your chosen system are powerful enough to suit the needs of your users today, as well as in the future.

Multi-tasking Processes

IBM mainframes are multi-tasking. That is, they can run multiple programs and tasks simultaneously, with each receiving a slice of CPU time. The operating system manages all the activity and protects each task from invasion by the others. Ordinarily this has no more significance to an on-line text system than it does to any other system. However, you should investigate the possibility of exploiting multi-tasking to improve the performance of your on-line text system. This exploitation can take two forms:

- Shared code

- Parallel processes

One of the advantages to multi-tasking operating systems is that program code, if written correctly, can be shared between users. This can dramatically improve performance, because each user needs much less storage. Systems of the sort we are describing can involve quite a lot of program code that must either be fully resident in memory or must be swapped in and out as needed. Such systems are also typically executed by many people simultaneously, which provides an excellent opportunity for sharing code.

For code to be shared in this manner it must be *re-entrant*, and it must be installed into the shared code area of your operating system.

Multi-tasking can be exploited to provide parallel processing for individual users, or at least the illusion of parallel processing. IBM computers are capable of some parallel processing, but it requires quite sophisticated programming and does not happen automatically. It is possible for on-line text systems to *hand off* search processes and other long-term procedures to other tasks while allowing the user to continue performing useful work. Formatting is another task that can be handed to a subtask started just for that purpose. Investigate the possibility of such features for your system.

Graphics

In terms of processor impact, graphics can be a killer. IBM mainframes have very inefficient graphics handling systems and can be brought to their knees by **heavy** graphics systems. Some of this workload can be offloaded into distributed function terminals such as the 3179-G or 3192-G, and even more can be turned over to PS/2s operating as graphics workstations, but the host still performs a lot of calculations. Be prepared for this if you implement a graphics-based on-line text system. Some improvement can be achieved by pre-building some graphics and displaying them in static form, but this reduces some of the flexibility of graphics as well.

You might consider generating and displaying the graphics in a window of a workstation system rather than in the mainframe's 3270 window. This approach can certainly offload the graphics-processing requirement from the host, but you do need very sophisticated software to tie multiple workstations together, probably into a Local Area Network, in order to share non-host resident graphics.

In general, you will find that graphics (and WYSIWYG, discussed below) generate the largest processor load for an on-line text system.

WYSIWYG

It is simply not feasible to attempt What-You-See-Is-What-You-Get text displays on an IBM host-based environment without workstations. The 3270 architecture is not designed for the data load or the processing requirements. However, all is not lost. Workstations that can perform the appropriate font loading and scaling directly, without being a burden to the host, can serve the WYSIWYG needs.

Even so, WYSIWYG is much harder to implement and support in a timely fashion than the use of standard screen fonts for text display. All of the issues discussed in this chapter, such as page transition time and multi-tasking must be reconsidered in the light of a decision to support WYSIWYG.

This raises an issue for designers: must all users have WYSIWYG capability, or can some do without? If only some users need it, but many do not, the system must be prepared to support both types of display with minimal impact on host performance. This may involve the software managing multiple versions of the text. Be sure all these considerations have been examined and dealt with before implementation.

We have found that, while WYSIWYG is very nice and certainly flashy, there are very few real-world business applications that *require* it. Be sure yours is one of them before you expend a lot of time, energy, money, and CPU resources providing facilities that are not necessary.

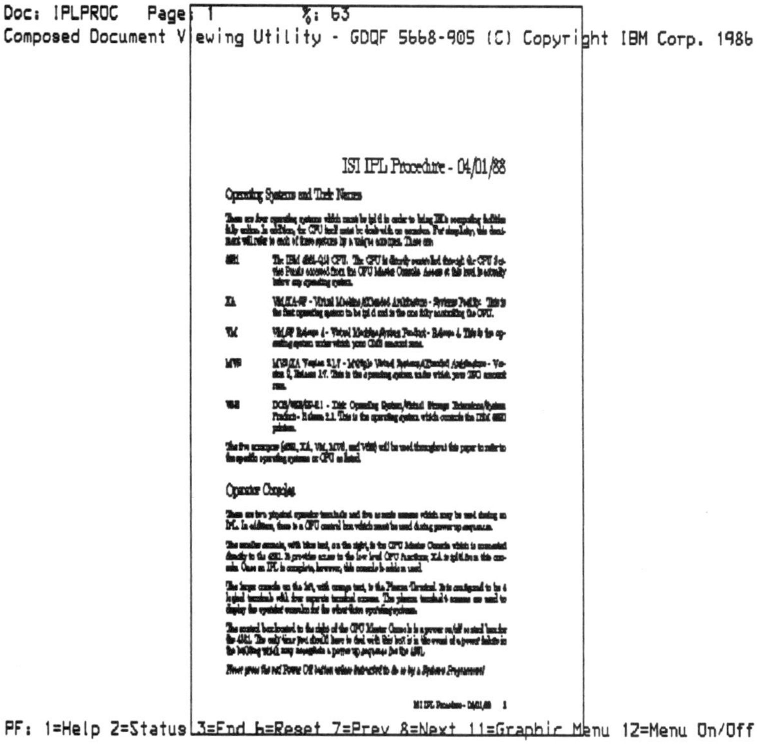

Figure 16-1. CDVU panel from an 8514 monitor on a PS/2: This example was captured from a Composed Document Viewing Utility screen displayed on a PS/2 8514 monitor, the highest resolution monitor available to be attached to the mainframe.

Appendices

Appendix

Evaluation Checklist Review

In *Evaluation Checklist* on page 99 we introduced some questions that we suggested as a basis for investigating your environment to determine how an on-line text display system might work in your environment and what resources were available to put the system in place. Our intent in this appendix is to help point you in a direction if you are uncertain about what the answers you found may mean for you. Remember that these are only pointers, not final answers.

1. **What are your publishing requirements?**

    - **Memos/letters:** If this is your only requirement, consider using a page makeup system on a PC. You probably do not need a complex mainframe-based system. If, however, this is only one of your requirements, and you would like to build a textbase of memos and letters which can be accessed using on-line display techniques, be sure that the system designers are aware of this requirement in advance so that they can design appropriate display environments.
    - **Policy and procedures manuals for in-house distribution:** This will require that all in-house users have access to a terminal or a PC acting as a terminal. Balance this cost against the benefit of access to the material. Remember that the cost of the terminals and any additional hardware required to make this access available may be offset by your current cost to reprint and distribute your in-house manuals.

- **Marketing material:** Your considerations here are typically the same as for memos and letters, although it is rarely necessary to have on-line access to marketing material.
- **User guides and reference materials associated with vendor products:** Check with your vendors to determine if they can provide on-line documents to you. If they can, factor in the cost of providing terminals to your users and the savings in purchasing fewer copies of the manuals from the vendor and the distribution of those manuals. You may find that this is a viable alternative to paper manuals. However, if the vendors do not provide on-line documentation, and you are not already engaged in providing site-specific documentation to your users pertaining to vendor products, it may not be feasible to provide vendor documentation on-line.
- **User guides and reference materials created for use with products developed in-house:** This is where the greatest control is available. You are already expending an effort to produce documents and distribute them. By moving to an on-line environment you can streamline the document creation, distribution, and updating cycles.
- **User guides and reference materials created for use with products developed for sale:** Here the considerations include what value you can add to your product by providing an on-line document system to your users. You may find that the same considerations involved in evaluating in-house on-line document production form the basis of selling the concept to your market.

2. **How much do you currently spend to create documents in-house?**

   If your current costs are negligible, and the number of documents you product is small, on-line display will not significantly change your bottom line. The exception would be if you are looking to distribute on-line documentation with a product you manufacture. In that case you should look not so much at the cost of your current document production as the value to be added to your product if you provide on-line documentation with it.

   If your costs are high, look seriously at where those costs are incurred. If you determine that most of it is maintaining personnel to create documents, and not in the reproduction and distribution, then on-line document display will not significantly reduce your costs. The more money you currently spend on reproduction and distribution, the more likely it is that an on-line display system for your text will provide a cost savings.

3. **Which publishing requirements would you like to satisfy with an on-line text application?**

   - Faster revision and distribution of documents
   - Increased availability of written material
   - Increased usability of written material
   - Less expensive distribution

   All of these are possible. Remember that your document production environment is what determines the speed of the availability of new information, even in the on-line environment. If you cannot put procedures in place which ensure the speed of updates being placed in production, the on-line text display system cannot provide many of its possible benefits.

4. **What type of text access best suits your environment?**

   - Application-based entry into a complex system of related text members
   - Context-sensitive entry into a complex system of related text members
   - Context-sensitive entry into a complex system of unrelated text members

   Remember that the sophistication of programming required increases as you move down the list. Design a system that meets your needs, and the needs of your users, but is not over-engineered for the environment.

5. **How sophisticated are your users?**
   Are they:

   - Afraid of the computer system?
   - People who will use only the functions necessary to do their own job?
   - Casual users of single applications?
   - Regular users of personal computing environments?
   - People who will use any system to its fullest?
   - People who enjoy learning and using new technology?

The more comfortable your users are with technology, the more likely it is that your on-line text display system will gain acceptance. Educate those that are afraid of the computer, and encourage your casual users to become more involved with what is available in your computer environment.

6. **Acceptable length of time for training users?**
    For those who are:

    - Afraid of the computer system: several months
    - People who will use only the functions necessary to do their own job: several weeks
    - Casual users of single applications: a week
    - Regular users of personal computing environments: a week
    - People who will use any system to its fullest: a few days
    - People who enjoy learning and using new technology: a few days

    If you do not allow for a learning curve and continued training your users will suffer and be less likely to accept the new system.

7. **What is your current MIS environment?**

    - **In-house or service bureau?** Service bureau environments make it harder to create and implement any new type of application system for in-house use since it is often hard to justify the expense incurred as development cost. We would recommend an in-house environment as a minimum requirement.
    - **Operating system?**
        - VM?
        - MVS?
        - VSE?
        - A combination? If so, where does the text composition function normally reside?

        It is important that the development of an in-house text display system be done in the principal environment in which it is intended to run so that the developers understand the environment to be used by the users. We consider VM to be the ideal environment, although MVS has many attractive facilities.
    - **How many applications do you currently use?**

The greater the number of applications, the more you may find yourself confronting users who are not willing to learn still another unless you can prove that it will make their life easier. This is where investigating the availability of on-line documents from your application vendors may prove to be a selling point. If all applications were developed in-house, however, the selling points should emphasize the speed of information access.

Another factor to consider is that if your environment is already using its hardware and software at maximum levels, it may not be able to support the development or implementation of another application system, such as on-line text display.

- **How much interactive computing does your shop provide?**
  ° Very little?
  ° TSO or CMS?
  ° Personal Computers also serving as mainframe terminals?

  If there is not an interactive computing facility currently available, you will require one before an on-line text display system can be implemented.

- **How much of your current data processing resources are currently consumed?**

  The higher your daily resource consumption in relation to your CPU capacity, the harder it will be to add the on-line text display system to your environment without impacting all other applications.

8. **Are you restricted to using existing hardware or can you purchase new hardware?**

   - **No budget available:** On-line text display is probably out of your reach.
   - **Budget requests must be made one year or more in advance:** Plan carefully, looking at your actual document production and distribution costs and present a business case to the management. This book gives you the tools to make an intelligent and viable presentation if on-line text display is warranted for your environment.
   - **Money is made available based on demonstrated need:** Same as above, although your chance of putting a

system in place which can begin saving money on document reproduction and distribution quickly is better.
- **Purchases require approval from management more than one level higher** Extensive planning and an excellent business case are normally required to get approval from management removed from the activity, but with a good business plan and carefully researched answers to questions about the actual cost benefits and productivity benefits, it should be possible to sell this project.

9. **Can your data processing resources be expanded?**

- Processing resources
- Storage
- Terminals and displays

If they cannot be expanded and your capacity is close to its limit, on-line text display is probably not possible. The greater your capability to expand, both in the type of hardware and amount of storage, the greater your chance of implementing a successful on-line text display system.

10. **How sophisticated is your hardware environment?**
    Do the end users have:

- Monochrome displays
- Color displays
- Color displays with graphics capability
- High resolution color graphics displays
- Access to both PC and host-based programs
- Access to both PC and host from one workstation
- Access to information stored on-line, near-line, and off-line without intervention by a systems person?

Remember that the less sophisticated terminals rope you into a less sophisticated text display environment. If graphics are a consideration, look carefully to see if your current environment can support it. As a minimum, we would suggest that the heaviest users of the on-line text display system be upgraded to some type of color monitor with some type of graphics capability.

11. **What type of terminals will users have?**

- Monochrome displays attached only to the mainframe
- Color displays attached only to the mainframe

- Color displays with graphics capability attached only to the mainframe
- High resolution color graphics displays attached only to the mainframe
- Any of the above also attached to a PC or a LAN

The considerations here are the same as above.

12. **Will all users have their own terminals?**

    - Each user has a personal terminal
    - Users share terminal access within a work group

    We recommend that all users have their own terminals.

13. **What are your allowable development costs?**

    - Some percentage of existing revenues
    - Some percentage of projected revenues
    - Some percentage of anticipated savings
    - Flat dollar amount based on current estimating formulas

    Use this figure to carefully determine what you can develop for that amount of money. If you cannot get the system you need, petition your management for what you need. Do not build only half a system and try to make do. Half a system is more frustrating and more detrimental to employee productivity that any company needs to deal with.

14. **What are your allowable operating expenses after completion?**

    - Some percentage of existing revenues
    - Some percentage of projected revenues
    - Some percentage of anticipated savings
    - Flat dollar amount based on current estimating formulas

    Be sure that everyone involved understands that the on-line text display system will have maintenance costs and that the cost of upkeep and the manpower to ensure the upkeep are mandatory.

15. **What is your allowable resource usage after completion?**

    - Support personnel
    - Maintenance personnel
    - CPU and DASD consumption

Ensure that these figures are derived and presented to your management and your staff so that all of the people involved understand that the new system has some overhead associated with it.

16. **What is the acceptable length of time for development and implementation?**

    - **Less than one year:** Consider purchasing a shell
    - **One to two years:** Realistic
    - **More than two years** Prone to over-engineering

17. **What is the acceptable length of time for training maintenance programmers?**

    - If the programmer was part of the project, no training time should be required
    - For a new programmer, assume at least two months

    Do not, however, forget that these people do need to be trained and kept up-to-date on any changes to the system.

Appendix

B

Creating This Book

This book was created using many of the tools described within its pages. Although the book itself is not available in an on-line form, much of the writing utilized on-line text facilities available in our shop. Many times, our ability to view, edit, revise, and correct the text using on-line facilities made the writing much easier and produced, we hope, a better written book.

Our On-line Environment

The computing environment used to write this book consisted of:

- An IBM 4381 mainframe computing system with 32 GB of DASD storage attached to it. Not all this storage was available to us, but we had access to as much as we needed and more.

- The operating system was IBM's VM/SP and its interactive computing component, CMS. We each had our own CMS account, two minidisks for CMS files, and as much as 16 MB of virtual storage. Typically, each of our virtual machines ran with 4 MB of virtual storage.

- The CMS XEDIT full-screen editor was invaluable. In addition to its excellent text editing facilities, it also offers the power typing facility, which allows easy entry of large quantities of text, and a host of utility macros such as the *ALL* macro that displays only the lines meeting specified criteria, then limits editing scope to only those lines. XEDIT screen management facilities, under the control of macros, also provided the facility for rapid prototyping of some on-line text systems discussed in the book. These will be explored in *Our On-line Environment* on page 225.

- IBM's Document Composition Facility provided the electronic typesetting capability that allowed us to do several things.

  ○ Rapidly produce draft copies for off-line editing and review

  ○ Experiment with style changes to optimize the appearance of the text

  ○ Produce versions of the text for on-line viewing using the same source text that produced the printed versions

  ○ Produce a final output file in the PostScript language for shipment directly to the book publisher. This file was then used to produce the camera-ready masters for printing the book you now hold.

- IBM's GDDM and its utilities were used to create most graphics. The Interactive Chart Utility was used for many of the graphics. Others were created with a modified version of ADMUSP4 which we call GRAFEDIT. ADMUSP4 is a sample graphics editor IBM distributes with GDDM. We have modified it to directly produce IBM Page Segments for DCF or to produce bitmaps which can be turned into PostScript images with a utility program we wrote. Several graphics were also created by scanning images to create bitmaps, and then transforming the bitmap into a PostScript image.

- IBM 3820 printers were used for printing some early drafts. Since the release of DCF we were using (3.2) can produce PostScript, we also draft printed on a QMS/PS 800+ PostScript printer. Ultimately, PostScript output was copied to a disk and shipped to the publisher for use on a PrintWare PostScript printer. This allowed us to produce draft print which was identical in style and fonts to the final book, and then get the higher resolution required for book publishing.

- IBM 3179-G terminals were used for editing, on-line text display, and graphics creation. In addition, some of the graphics were created using an IBM PS/2 Model 60 with the 3270 Workstation program. We discovered that running GRAF-EDIT on this terminal enabled functions in the program which were unavailable on 3179-Gs.

This computing environment is very well suited to the task of book writing, editing, and publishing, but is not the optimal one described for on-line text management. It is very close, however, and supported one of the most interesting tasks we undertook while writing the book.

Appendix

Creating a Prototype On-line Text Environment

As we were researching the subject of on-line text access and management, we discovered that we needed more immediate experience with a HyperText system on an IBM mainframe to write definitely about it. To learn more, we took about a month out of the writing schedule to create a HyperText prototype on the mainframe. To accomplish our goals, we had to develop several pieces of new software:

- An XEDIT-based window display environment already existed from previous research. We modified it to better support our needs, and then incorporated it into the Hypertext prototype.

- A DCF profile was developed to format text for the window environment. The goal was to be able to use the same source text for both the HyperText environment and output to any of a variety of printers.

- DCF macros were developed to automatically define Hypertext link information. These macros also had to disable themselves when the output destination was not the HyperText environment.

- Several display strategies were explored, including:

    ° 45-column windows

- Small windows requiring left-right scrolling
- Tiled window placement
- Intelligent overlapping window placement
- Random overlapping window placement
- Pseudo-random window placement
- 65-column windows
- 80-column windows
- Full-screen background window with smaller secondary windows
- Variable-size windows
- Windows and text matched to provide windowed pagination
- Free-flowing text to eliminate pagination in windows

The prototype system we settled on used:

- 45-column windows
- 45-character text lines; no left-right scrolling required
- Pseudo-random overlapping window placement
- Unpaginated text: headings and paragraph breaks had blank lines separating them, but there were no running headings or footings

We determined that it was necessary to produce a post-processor which would resolve linkage information produced during the composition step into a true HyperText linkage database. This program, like all the other program code we wrote, was in CMS REXX for rapid development and change. The final link database was relational in structure, but was accessed in a more associative manner by the system driver programs.

Displaying HyperText links and providing some form of HyperDocument Browser was accomplished using DCF macros which marked specific text as HyperText nodes. These nodes were displayed in a different color or intensity to provide users with visual clues to their importance. A function key was used to display a window with all the defined links for the HyperText node pointed to by the cursor position. When a link was selected, a new node was displayed in a window. The top line of the window displayed an information bar which explained where the node had been accessed from. Window placement also gave the user visual clues as to the linkage ordering.

Our Hypertext prototype was, by no means, a production-level system. Even as a prototype it had many defects which we did not correct after we identified them. Its importance to this book was that it allowed us to explore the issues relating to mainframe-based HyperText systems directly. By using CMS XEDIT screen drivers and CMS REXX program code, we were able to rapidly reprogram fundamental components to experiment with different options. This allowed us to investigate many different options for a HyperText system without a tremendous effort; the entire prototype except for the window display system was written, torn apart, and re-written many times in a single month of effort.

The next logical step would be to translate the prototype into a compiled language to improve the response time and portability of the HyperText environment.

Appendix

Trademarks

Many of the programs and products mentioned in this book are trademarks of their owning corporations. In this appendix we list each product by its common acronym and who owns its trademark or copyright.

For further information on any of the products cited, please contact the vendor directly. If you cannot locate the information you require, please contact the authors.

1. Adobe Systems, Inc., 1585 Charlton Rd, Box 7900, Mountain View, CA 94039-7900

    - PostScript

2. Applied Data Research (ADR), Orchard Road and Route 206, Princeton, NJ 08540

    - ETC
    - ROSCOE

3. AT&T, 550 Madison Ave., New York, NY 10022

    - UNIX

4. Goal Systems,Inc., 7965 North High Street, Columbus, OH 43235

    - Preference

229

5. Image Sciences, Inc., 5910 North Central Expressway, Suite 800, Dallas, TX 75206

   - DCF/Plus
   - DocuVise

6. Interleaf, Inc., 10 Canal Park, Cambridge, MA 02141

   - Interleaf

7. International Business Machines, Inc., Old Orchard Rd., Armonk, NY 10504

   - AFPDS
   - AIX
   - BookMaster
   - BrowseMaster
   - CDVU
   - CMS
   - DCF
   - DisplayWrite/370
   - DisplayWrite TextPak 4
   - FLSF
   - GDDM
   - IBM
   - ICCF
   - Interleaf Publisher
   - ISPF
   - ODF
   - OGL
   - PC-DOS
   - PDF
   - PMF
   - PPFA
   - PS/2
   - Publishing SolutionPac
   - TSO
   - VM/CFS
   - VSSE
   - XEDIT
   - 3820

8. MicroSoft, Inc., PO Box 97017, Redmond, WA 98073-9717

- MS-DOS
- XENIX

9. Sun Microsystems, Inc., 2500 Garcia Ave., Mountain View, CA 94043

- SunOS

10. QMS, Inc., 1 Magnum Pass, Mobile, AL 36618

- QUIC

11. Xerox Corporation, 800 Long Ridge Rd, Stamford, CT 06904

- HFDL
- metacode
- UDK
- XICS
- 9700, 9790, 8700, 8790, 4050

INDEX

A

A Programming Language
  (APL) 38
access method
  selection 94
access methods
  inverted list 185
  terminology 34
  text 178-179
  VSAM 34
  VTAM 34
access time
  DASD 27
  optical disk 27
Advanced Function Printing
  Data Stream (AFPDS) 35
annotation 18, 89, 144
  public vs. private 144
application error
  messages 72-74
artwork
  scanning 157
ASCII to EBCDIC
  conversion 31
Assembler Language Code
  (ALC) 37
associative indexing 85
associative navigation 84-86
  characteristics 84-86

B

bitmaps 30, 118
bookmark 87
bookmarks 89, 194
BrowseMaster 124
browser 190

C

C programming language 38
CD-ROM 25, 56
  storage capacity 26
color
  on screen 108
  screen design 110
command language 33
  REXX 34
Common Business Oriented
  Language (COBOL) 37
communications protocols 34
compilers and
  subprograms 37
Composed Document Viewing
  Utility (CDVU) 124
composition and printing
  terminology 35-37
computer-based
  instruction 79
content-based access
  methods 185
content-based search 86
context sensitive text
  access 7, 77

233

Conversational Monitor
  System (CMS)   34
    data organization   42
    library   43
    XEDIT   34
cooperative computing facilities   143
CPU load   102, 218
    cycles   30
    graphics   207-208
    multi-tasking
      processes   207
    page transition time   204
    search algorithms   205-206
    WYSIWYG   208
CPU power   51-54
Customer Information Control
  System (CICS)   34
    Interactive Computing and
      Control Facility
      (ICCF)   34

D

DASD   23, 25, 55
    access time   27
    3380 capacity   25
Data Language 1 (DL1)   39
data organization
    architecture   41
    MVS   41
    Partitioned Data Set
      (PDS)   42
    terminology   41-43
    VM   42
    VSAM-based   41
data structures
    partitioned data sets   180
    streamed records   182
    text   179-184
    typed records   181

variable length
  records   179
database management
  systems   39
    Data Language 1 (DL1)   39
    DB2   39
    Structured Query
      Language/Data System
      (SQL/DS)   39
database managers   183
database organization
    content-based   45
    DB2   44
    hierarchical   43
    IMS   43
    relational   44
    SQL/DS   44
    terminology   43-45
    VM Contextual File Search
      (VM/CFS)   45
Diconix UDK printers   36
displays   29-30, 102, 118, 218
    bitmapped   30
    megabit   29
    workstation   64
    5080   29
    8507   29
    8514   29
distribution   12, 16, 97
    costs   98
    enhancement   100, 215
document access   201-202
Document Composition
  Facility (DCF)   35, 153, 155,
  163
    AFPDS   35
    line printer output   35
    Office Document Feature
      (ODF)   153
    PostScript output   35
    profiles   117

document creation 12, 15, 18, 158, 170-174
  cost 100, 214
  methodology 13
  review 143
  traditional methods 20
document elements 88
document maintenance 116
document management 167
  naming conventions 168
  version control 169
document organization
  terminology 40-41
document signature
 indexing 86
  noise references 86
document structure 195-201
  browser 190
  linear 198
  network 198
  relational 198
  tree 196
DocuVise 170

E

education 17, 101, 103, 216, 220
electronic libraries 15
  connecting
   members 187-194
  development 116-119
  document access 201-202
  document
   structure 195-201
  maintenance 15
  physical
   organization 178-184
  relating members 187-194
  search and
   retrieval 184-185
  text access 177-185, 201-202
electronic mail 143
Entry Sequenced Data Sets (ESDS) 41
error messages 72-74
  ABENDs 72
  off-line 72
evaluation checklist 99-103
evaluation checklist
 review 213-220
Extended Text Composition (ETC) 35, 37, 155

F

Font Library Service Facility (FLSF) 36
fonts
  in screen design 110
  screen design 111, 134
formatting 119-128
  manual 122, 123
  on-line vs. printed 164
  profiles 162
  style files 162
  windows 125
  with DCF 117
Formula Translator (FORTRAN) 38
free-standing text 6
full-screen text editor
  PDF 33, 51
  VSSE/ICCF 51
  XEDIT 34, 51

G

Generalized Markup Language
  (GML)   163
Graphical Data Display
  Manager (GDDM)   39
    Composed Document
      Viewing Utility
      (CDVU)   124
    Presentation Graphics
      Feature (PGF)   39
graphics   90
  CPU load   207-208
  in composed text   173
  raster   62
  searches   85
  vector   62
graphics terminals   61-66
groupware   143

H

hardware
  budget   102, 217
  terminology   28-32
help
  tree structures   197
help systems   4-6
Host Forms Description
  Language (HFDL)   37
HyperDocument   40, 90
  organization   200
  video input   92
HyperMedia   40, 91-94, 147
  graphics   92
  storage media   92
  video input   92
HyperText   23, 40, 87-91, 127

annotation   89
bookmarks   89
definition   87
document elements   88
graphics   90
link types   88, 89
links   87, 88, 90, 188
nodes   90
relating documents   188

I

Information Management
  System (IMS)   34
    database organization   43
Interactive Chart Utility
  (ICU)   39
Interactive Computing and
  Control Facility (ICCF)   34
interactive computing environ-
  ment   101, 217
interactive computing environ-
  ments   50, 143
    terminology   33-34
interactive education   79
Interactive System Produc-
  tivity Facility (ISPF)   33
    Program Development
      Facility (PDF)   33
Interleaf Publisher   154

J

jukebox   26
  storage capacity   27

K

Key Sequenced Data Sets
  (KSDS) 42
keys 88, 89, 90, 184
keyword-based search 85, 86

L

linear document 40
linear text 84
link type 88, 89, 188
links 88, 90, 188
  bibliographies 192
  citations 192
  directed 188
  footnotes 192
  index 192
  network 188
  reference strategies 189
  table of contents 192
Local Area Network
  (LAN) 30, 64, 93
    gateway 30
Local Area Networks
  (LANs) 27

M

mainframe
  requirements 49-67
management
  considerations 11-21
metacode 37
migration planning 158
MS-DOS 32
multi-tasking processes 207
Multiple Virtual Storage
  (MVS) 32

Customer Information
Control System
  (CICS) 34
Time Sharing Option
  (TSO) 33

N

nd/annotation 146
near-line storage 28, 57, 202
  Automated Tape Library
    (ATL) 57
  Hierarchically Archived
    Datasets 57
networks 30-31
nodes 89, 90
non-linear document 40
non-linear text 87, 90

O

OCR scanners 31
OCR scanners (OCR)
  ASCII output 31
off-line storage 58-59
  optical tape 28
  tape 27
  terminology 27-28
Office Document Feature
  (ODF) 153
  RFTGML 154
on-line help 4-6, 73, 75
  tree structures 197
on-line storage 55-56
  terminology 25-27
on-line text access
  cost benefits 12, 16
  costs 13, 98
  development costs 103,
    219
  environments 9-10

238 On-line Text Management

evaluation   95-99, 213
implementation   11, 13, 51
justification   8-9, 12-17
library creation   15
library maintenance   15
operating costs   103, 219
other benefits   16
types   101, 215
users   17
on-line tutorials   77-78
operating system   49, 101, 216
   MS-DOS   32
   MVS   32
   PC-DOS   32
   UNIX   32
   VM   32
   VSE   32
Optical Character Recognition
 (OCR)   15, 31
   scanners   119, 156
optical disk   25, 56-57, 94
   access time   27
   CD-ROM   25
   lands   25
   pits   25
   storage cost   27
   WORM   25
organization
   terminology   39-47
overlapping windows   139
Overlay Generation Language
 (OGL)   36

P

Page Printer Formatting Aid
 (PPFA)   36
panels
   advantages   137
   defined   133
   disadvantages   137
   organization   137
   versus windows   137
Partitioned Data Set
 (PDS)   42, 180
PASCAL   38
PC-DOS   32
peripheral storage   25
personal computers
   as workstations   30
PostScript
   device independence   35
   font scaling   35
   produced by DCF   35
PostScript Display   35
Preference by Goal
 Systems   118
presentation   115-129
presentation control   131-143
Presentation Graphics Feature
 (PGF)   39
   Interactive Chart Utility
    (ICU)   39
Presentation Manager   131
presentation methods   82-84
Print Management Facility
 (PMF)   36
printer resolution   35
ProcessMaster   170
processor
 considerations   203-208
profiles   162
   selection at
    composition   163
Program Development Facility
 (PDF)   33, 51
   Library Management (LM)
    routines   39
Programming Language/1
 (PL/1)   38
PS/2 display   29
PU load   124
pull-down menus   84

Q

Query Management Facility (QMF) 39
QUIC printers 36

R

reference text 77
Relative Record Data Sets (RRDS) 42
requirements
  CPU 49
  full-screen text editor 51
  input devices 51
  interactive computing environment 50
  operating system 49
  publishing 100, 213
  storage 51
Restructure Executive Editor (REXX) 34, 38
Revisable Form Text Document Content Architecture (RFTDCA) 153, 155
revision cycles 15, 16, 20, 152, 158, 165
  enhancement 100, 215

S

scanners 31-32
  OCR 31, 156
  restrictions 156
scanning 15, 118, 156-158
  SEE ALSO text capture
  art 157-158
  photographs 158
screen
  fonts 108
  format 115-129
  transition 111
screen design 107-113, 127
  color 110
  depth 111-113, 126
  ease of use 142-143
  fonts 110-111, 134
  mixed-case text 110
  panels 133
  references 107
  restrictions 108-113
  size 108
  text 140-142
  use 134
  windows 132-133, 138-140
screen presentation 89, 131-143
  management 93
screen text
  mixed case 108
scrolling 112, 125, 142
search algorithms 205-206
  fuzzy search 206
  text 178
  tuning 206
security 20
software
  terminology 32-39
specific text mapping 74-76
storage
  cost 27
  CPU 54
  DASD 25
  disk drives 25
  evaluation 102, 218
  gigabytes 24
  kilobytes 24
  megabytes 24
  off-line 24
  on-line 24
  optical disk 25
  requirements 51, 54
  tape cartridges 28

tape drives 28
terabytes 24
terminology 24-28
text 151
virtual 24
storage capacity 28
storage requirements 59
Structured Query
  Language/Data System
  (SQL/DS) 39
style specifications 162
system organization
  command-driven 45
  menu-driven 45
  terminology 45-47
  window-driven 46
system planning 19, 95, 99,
  134, 213
Systems Application Architecture (SAA) 38
  Common User Access
    (CUA) 134
Systems Network Architecture
  (SNA) 34

T

tape cartridges 28
tape drives 28
terminals 29, 51, 60-66, 101,
  102, 118, 124, 131, 217, 218
  color 61
  fonts 64
  graphics 61-66
  high-resolution 93
  hot keys 113
  mixed case 110
  screen depth 111
  scrolling 112
  text-only 60-61
  types 108

window display 112
WYSIWYG 61-66
3270 emulators 110
terminology 23-47
text
  batch composition 35
  blinking 111
  commenting 166
  composition 123
  data structures 179
  database 154
  document
    management 167
  file creation 170
  file management 165
  file naming
    conventions 168
  file size 164
  footnotes 171
  formatting files 162
  formatting
    restrictions 107
  graphics 173
  highlighting uses 111
  main document file 167
  maintenance 152, 165
  mapping 74-76
  multi-column text 172
  references within 171
  reverse video 111
  screen design 140-142
  search algorithms 178
  source file
    configuration 161
  storage 151
  style specifications 162
  tabular material 172
  tracking updates 152
  unformatted 173
text access 18, 71-79, 201-202
  associative
    navigation 84-86

Index   241

cost benefits   16
costs   98
CPU load   203-208
definition   3-8
development costs   103, 219
electronic
  libraries   177-185
evaluation   95-99, 213
  goals   95
HyperText   87-91
in-memory documents   202
keyed   178
library creation   15
library maintenance   15
near-line storage   202
new methods   81-94
non-keyed   178
on-demand   85
on-line environments   9-10
operating costs   103, 219
other benefits   16
search and
  retrieval   184-185
types   4-7, 101, 215
users   17
text capture   116-119, 153
  SEE ALSO scanning
  copying   117
  cost   153
  from floppy disk   154
  from host files   154
  keying   116, 156
text display   171
text formatting   119-128, 152
  consistency   129
  graphic   125
  maintenance   123
  manual   122, 123
  on-line vs. printed   164
  windows   127
  with DCF   117

text library
  evaluation   151-159
  existing   152-155
  new   155-156
  size   158
text perusal   143-147
Time Sharing Option
  (TSO)   33
  CLIST   33
  Interactive System Productivity Facility (ISPF)   33
tuning   54
tutorials   77-78

U

UDK printers
  Diconix Dijit 1   36
  Xerox 3700   36
  Xerox 4045   36
UNIX   32
user interface   94, 101, 215

V

version control   169
  DocuVise   170
  ProcessMaster   170
Virtual Machine (VM)   32, 34
  Conversational Monitor
    System (CMS)   34
virtual storage   24, 54-55
  address space   24
  terminology   24-25
Virtual Storage Extended
  (VSE)   34
  Customer Information
    Control System
    (CICS)   34
Virtual Storage Extensions
  (VSE)   32

VM Contextual File Search
  (VM/CFS) 45
VSAM 34
  ESDS 41
  keys 184
  KSDS 41
  RRDS 41
VSSE/ICCF 51
VTAM 34

W

windows 82, 112, 125
  advantages 134
  components 132
  defined 132-133
  design 138-140
  desktop paradigm 82
  disadvantages 134
  formatting 125, 127
  organization 137
  overlapping 139
  pop-up menus 46
  pull-down menus 46
  screen design 134
  scrolling 125
  size 135
  tiling 46, 138, 140
  versus panels 137
workstations 30, 110
WORM 25, 56
  jukebox 26
  storage capacity 26
WYSIWYG 29, 124, 208
WYSIWYG terminals 63

X

XEDIT 34, 51
Xerox Integrated Composition
  System (XICS) 35, 155
  metacode 36
Xerox metacode printers 37
Xerox UDK printers
  3700 36
  4045 36

DATE DUE			
GAYLORD			PRINTED IN U.S.A